How to Get on

JEOPARDY!

. . . and Win!

How to Get on

JEOPARDY!

. . . and Win!

VALUABLE INFORMATION
FROM A CHAMPION

Michael Dupée

A Citadel Press Book
Published by Carol Publishing Group

To the woman to whom I have already dedicated
my life and love, Zana Holley

A Citadel Press Book
Published by Carol Publishing Group
Citadel Press is a registered trademark of Carol Communications, Inc.

Editorial, sales and distribution, rights and permissions inquiries should be
addressed to Carol Publishing Group, 120 Enterprise Avenue, Secaucus, N.J.
07094.

In Canada: Canadian Manda Group, One Atlantic Avenue, Suite 105, Toronto,
Ontario M6K 3E7

Carol Publishing Group books may be purchased in bulk at special discounts for
sales promotion, fund-raising, or educational purposes. Special editions can be
created to specifications. For details, contact Special Sales Department, Carol
Publishing Group, 120 Enterprise Avenue, Secaucus, N.J. 07094.

Manufactured in the United States of America

10 9 8 7 6 5 4 3 2 1

Library of Congress Cataloging-in-Publication Data

Dupée, Michael.
    How to get on Jeopardy and win : valuable information from a
champion / Michael Dupée.
        p. cm.
    "A Citadel Press Book."
    ISBN 0-8065-1991-6 (pb)
    1. Jeopardy (Television program)   I. Title.
PN1992.77.J363D86   1998
791.45'72—dc21   98-26500
                                                        CIP

CONTENTS

PREFACE

Even "Burt" Watches the Show

At a gas station off I-75 in Micanopy, Florida, I first realized just how popular *Jeopardy!* really is. It was the day after the final show of the 1996 Tournament of Champions aired, and I stopped for gas after many hours on the road. The owner of the station was a burly man wearing the traditional oil-stained blue jeans and work shirt, complete with a patch bearing his name— "BURT." When we first came up to pay, he just gave us a quick nod and took my credit card, but then he read my name and quickly looked up at me. A big smile came over his face, and he stuck out his hand and gushed, "Son, I just gotta shake your hand. Wait 'til I tell the missus that I saw you."

They never missed the show at home, he said, though he did not always know the answers. I was astounded. Who would have expected an auto mechanic in a rural gas station to watch the show, or the inner-city teenagers who two days later shyly approached me for an autograph? It was amazing: cashiers, lawyers, clerks, firefighters, criminal defendants, doctors, doll-house makers, and many other shapes and sizes of people would get that "Hmm, how do I know that guy?" look and come over and ask me a million questions. "What is Alex *really* like? How can I get on the show? Did they tell you in advance what categories you would get? Did you pay a lot of taxes on that? Did you get to meet Vanna White?"

Two Types of *Jeopardy!* Fans That Will Love This Book

I noticed, too, that there are two types of *Jeopardy!* fans out there. One type, comprising most of the seventeen million people who watch the show every night, tunes in simply to be fascinated, entertained, humored, and impressed by the Emmy Award–winning questions, the savoir faire of Alex Trebek, and the astounding range of knowledge of some of America's smartest people. While these fans love the show, they are not planning to try out any time soon. But this does not stop them from being curious about what really happens behind the scenes and about what it takes to get on the show and win.

Especially curious, though, is the other type of fan—people who have always dreamed about being on the show. When I meet one of these fans, I know I am in for a barrage of questions. Luckily, I like talking about the show almost as much as I liked being on it, and, I must admit, I was just as curious when I was preparing to go on. The problem then was that I could not find a single-volume source which contained all the information I wanted to know and was written from a contestant's point of view. The wonderful books written by the *Jeopardy!* people themselves have some background information and lots of practice questions but do not focus on the contestant's point of view. Some other *Jeopardy!* and trivia books are long on facts but short on practical hints about what you will face when you hit that sound stage. This book is a bonanza of useful tips, *Jeopardy!* facts, behind-the-scenes accounts, and lots of fun trivia questions to test you.

So whether you are planning to take the *Jeopardy!* exam soon or only to take the *Jeopardy!* journey in your imagination, this is the place to start. I hope that you enjoy the book and find it informative. Most of all, I hope that it helps you win lots of *Jeopardy!*'s money!

Jeopardy! Trivia

Answers these trivial teasers about the show itself:

1. He invented *Jeopardy!* and had friends try playing it in his Manhattan apartment.
2. He hosted the show during its original run on NBC.
3. Who was the original and who is the current announcer (not host) for the show?
4. Who composed the *Jeopardy!* theme song?
5. When *Jeopardy!* was created, it was her idea to give the answers first and have the contestants supply questions.
6. In what subject did Alex Trebek get a college degree?
7. This New York transit cop won the most in a single five-game stint on *Jeopardy!*—over $102,000.
8. In 1993, the New York transit cop mentioned in question number 7 won the Jeopardy! Tenth Anniversary Tournament by knowing the name of the woman playwright who wrote *The Heidi Chronicles*. Later, the playwright actually called him for a date, and they went out. Who was that playwright?
9. What is the most money you can win in one show (assuming that you could keep everything)?
10. Jerome Vered won the most in a single game. Within $500, how much did he win?

Answers on page xiv.

ACKNOWLEDGMENTS

There are so many people involved in the making of a book, it doesn't seem fair that only one name goes on the cover. My first wish would be to thank the fans of *Jeopardy!* who have let me know that they enjoy my behind-the-scenes accounts, both in person and on the Internet.

The staff at Carol Publishing Group is amazing. In particular, I'd like to thank Gordon Allen, who had the idea for this book, publisher Steve Schragis, who asked me to write it, and Mike Lewis, who shepherded the project through with grace and dedication. Others who deserve mention are Diane Chin, Karen Quinn, and Renata Butera.

My family—wife Zana Holley, daughter Zadia Dupée, parents Doris and George Dupée, sisters and their husbands Judy and Brian Schweickart and Debi and Bill Hall—have in general looked kindly upon my "trivia-centric" life and, through a lifetime of game-playing, trained me for the show. For that, I'm grateful.

I also must thank my mentor, best friend, and fellow trivia lover, Jeff Gilden. He taught me many things about life, but most important, he taught me that knowledge is cool. Finally, I am forever indebted to my teachers and quiz bowl coaches, particularly two: Miss Erickson, for first noticing my fascination with trivia, and Lloyd Busch, for instilling in me an unabashed love of knowledge and for teaching me how to win.

INTRODUCTION

Welcome to *How to Get on* Jeopardy!...*and Win!*, the game show reference for those who want all the basics covered in one easy-to-use book.

Now, you have it. The tryouts. The interviews. What to study. Not to mention what to wear and how to pack. All in one place.

Whether you're looking to try out or wanting to learn all the behind-the-scenes information, this book contains something for you.

So make yourself comfortable and enjoy this comprehensive and easy-to-follow book *for Jeopardy!* lovers *from a Jeopardy!* lover.

You Don't Have to Be Rain Man to Win on *Jeopardy!*

Most people seem to think that to be on *Jeopardy!*, much less to be a *Jeopardy!* champion, you must be born with a freakish ability to memorize the annual rainfall amounts of the Amazon River basin on one reading or that you must have spent your entire life with your face stuck in a book. I'm here to tell you that neither of these is required, and, in fact, they might even be detrimental. What you *really* need to get on the show—and then win—are five things: a winning attitude, good luck, perseverance, smart preparation, and, of course, this book.

How This Book Is Organized

This book is divided into three sections, which will take you step-by-step through the *Jeopardy!* experience, from getting an initial tryout to playing like a winner during your games and even to filing your taxes after your victory. Plus, you'll learn tons of secrets about the show that most people don't know. You'll read behind-the-scenes accounts of *Jeopardy!* champions that will make you feel like you've been to the sound stage yourself, and you'll pick up tasty bits of trivia about *Jeopardy!* and its people. Finally, you'll learn what *Jeopardy!* is most likely to ask, and you'll hone your skills on thousands of questions.

Part 1: Getting on the Show. How do I get a tryout? Don't I have to beat out thousands of other hopefuls? How can I maximize my chances of being picked? What happens behind the scenes at the studio? What is the "greenroom"? Learn a few simple techniques that can give you a leg up on the competition.

Part 2: Playing Like a Champion. More questions—How do I use the buzzer? Is there a smart way to phrase your responses? What is the best way to bet on Daily Doubles? What is the "rule of two-thirds"? How should I bet in Final Jeopardy?—and the information you need to answer them. Then you'll learn everything you need know to play like a champ, including how to pick the next question when you are in control of the board.

Part 3: Learning the facts. All the facts that *Jeopardy!* loves to ask for again and again are outlined here, along with tips on evaluating your strong and weak areas. Have some fun practicing with over five thousand questions in *Jeopardy!* categories that I used to prepare myself to go on the show.

In this book, I will refer to the *Jeopardy!* clues as "questions" and to the questions supplied by contestants as "answers." *Jeopardy!* fans all know that the *Jeopardy!* clues are supposed to be the answers to the questions, which are supplied by the contestants; however, this can be rather confusing when discussing how to play the game. Thus, for clarity's sake, I have decided to use the traditional question-and-answer format to discuss the game.

I invite you to let me know about your *Jeopardy!* experiences and your tales of trying out for the show. You can read the exploits of other contestants as part of the Unofficial *Jeopardy!* Fan Club Newsletter, which is sent out monthly via e-mail. Sign up for a free subscription online at http://www.MindFun.com

My e-mail address is tikha@gator.net, but "snail mail" is just as nice to get at:

Michael Dupée
Trivia Mania
P.O. Box 2521
Gainesville, FL 32602

Answers to *Jeopardy!* Trivia

1. Merv Griffin invented *Jeopardy!*—and *Wheel of Fortune*.
2. Art Fleming was the original host.
3. Don Pardo was the original, and Johnny Gilbert is the announcer now.
4. Merv Griffin himself composed the "Final Jeopardy" theme.
5. Merv's wife, Julianne. It was a joking reference to the game show scandals of the 1950s in which players were given the "answers."
6. Alex Trebek has a degree in philosophy. He's no intellectual slouch.
7. Frank Spangenberg. However, neither Frank nor Chuck Forrest has won the most on the show. That honor belongs to Bob Blake, who won $182,501.
8. Wendy Wasserstein called Frank Spangenberg, and the two went on a date in Queens. Ms. Wasserstein wrote a story about it in which she notes that Frank was recognized much more often than she was.
9. $273,200. You would have to get every question and get the Daily Doubles in the $100 and $200 squares as the last square of each round.
10. $34,000.

PART I

Getting on the Show

This section explains how to get the tryout that thousands of others want and how to maximize your chances to make the cut once you are there. Then you'll get a behind-the-scenes look at what happens once you reach the studio and the mysterious "greenroom." Learn a few simple techniques that can give you a leg up on the competition.

CHAPTER 1

Getting a Tryout

We Love *Jeopardy!*

Since you picked up this book, you obviously love *Jeopardy!* You are not alone. *Jeopardy!* is the number-two-rated syndicated game show of all time (beaten only by *Wheel of Fortune*). It is watched by over seventeen million people every night, and a version of *Jeopardy!* is aired in a dozen different countries. The critics love the show too. Its writers and producers have won a staggering thirteen Emmys (maybe more by the time you read this).

Not only does it have great ratings, *Jeopardy!* is a cultural icon. Every day somebody somewhere answers something in the form of a question, and I bet 80 percent of people stopped on the street could hum the "Final Jeopardy!" theme. What's even more amazing is how often *Jeopardy!* is alluded to in movies and TV shows. Who can forget Cliff Claven's glorious flameout on *Jeopardy!* during a *Cheers* episode? How about Rosie Perez knowing seven foods that start with the letter *Q* in *White Men Can't Jump?* My favorite was *Pinky and the Brain,* in which Brain (called Brian by Alex Quebec) appeared on the show *Gyp-parody.* He knew all the questions in the category "Kings Named Moeshoeshoe" but could not identify Ralph Kramden's most

Shows and Movies That Have Featured
Scenes From *Jeopardy!*

Cheers

Who can forget poor Cliff, who knew everything about beer and stamps but nothing about betting strategy?

Rain Man

Raymond could not make change for a dollar but whipped through a whole category.

White Men Can't Jump

The "q"uintessential *Jeopardy!* contestant, Rosie Perez knew seven foods that started with the letter Q.

Groundhog Day

Bill Murray, living the same day over and over again, answers some of the questions even before they are asked.

Gone Fishin'

Two yokels, Joe Pesci and Danny Glover, watch the show and get no questions right. "Man, if you took history and literature off that show, I'd win," they later say.

The Nanny

Fran makes it onto the show and gets only questions dealing with fashion, shopping, and her recent vacation to Israel.

Pinky and the Brain

Brain gets every question on the board but misses Final *Jeopardy!* because he didn't listen to poor Pinky.

famous retort. (By the way, kings named Moeshoeshoe really existed, ruling Lesotho in southern Africa.)

As you read this book, you will quickly see that I am a *Jeopardy!* nut, so I admit that right up front. While I was growing up, at my house everything stopped at 7:30, when *Jeopardy!* came on. We all sat around the television shouting out answers and having a great time. And any chance we got, we played games like *Jeopardy!*, Trivial Pursuit, *Sale of the Century*, Scattegories, Taboo, *$25,000 Pyramid*, and even some we made up ourselves. Though we were just having fun, when I look back I realize it was almost like I'd spent my whole life practicing to be on the show. Over the years, I watched and analyzed *Jeopardy!* with more than just a fan's interest, for I always harbored the secret belief that I could make it onto the show and win.

Does that sound familiar? If it does, even vaguely, maybe you should try out for the show. Here are ten signs that you are ready for *Jeopardy!* stardom.

Top Ten Signs You Should Try Out for *Jeopardy!*

10. The organist played the "Final Jeopardy!" theme at your wedding.

 9. You have three *Jeopardy!* Challenges so everyone in your family can play along at home.

 8. No one will play Trivial Pursuit with you, ever, especially for money.

 7. It takes you half an hour to look a word up in the dictionary because you start browsing through it.

 6. You named your goldfish Thiamine, Niacin, and Riboflavin as a third grader.

 5. People call you up out of the blue to ask you about President Zachary Taylor.

 4. You named one of your children after Alex Trebek.

 3. You are a lawyer, schoolteacher, or free-lance writer.

 2. Your VCR is permanently set to record *Jeopardy!*

and the number 1 sign that you should try out for *Jeopardy!*:

 1. What is ...you *always* answer in the form of a question, even during job interviews.

...So How Do We Get on the Show?

An embarrassing number of the top ten signs applied to me, and I knew I was ready to go on the show. So I did some research. When it comes to getting onto America's favorite quiz show, the news is good and bad. First the bad news: it takes lots of perseverance, smarts, and luck. Every year, twenty-five-thousand prospective contestants take the *Jeopardy!* fifty-question written test and only 10 percent pass it, thereby moving on to the the mock game and interview portion of the tryout (more about that in chapter 2). Of the 2,500 that pass, only around four hundred are picked to be contestants each season. What's more, the twenty-five-thousand figure represents only those who got to take the test. Just think about all the people who sent in postcards, tried to call the participating radio station, or did whatever to try to get a shot at it. For example, at the television station in Cleveland where I tried out, they told us that they got six thousand postcards for the three hundred slots to take the test. So even getting a tryout is tough.

But there is good news, especially since you have this book. First, if you have been the returning champion dozens of times from the comfort of your easy chair and are going to bust if you don't get a tryout, take heart. You are guaranteed to get a chance.

You Are Guaranteed a Tryout, If You Just Gotta Get One

All you have to do is go to Los Angeles or Atlantic City. In Los Angeles, tests are conducted in the studio several times a month, and all you have to do is set up an appointment. For information on how to schedule a chance to take the test, write to:

> *Jeopardy!* Contestants
> Sony Pictures Studios
> 10202 West Washington Blvd.
> Culver City, CA 90232

or call Luci at *Jeopardy!*: (310) 244-5367

In their letter back to you, the *Jeopardy!* contestant coordinators will advise you not hike out to L.A. just to take the test, and I will do the same here. The chance of making it is not worth the expense, and there are many other ways to try out that have much better odds. But if you're out there anyway, definitely arrange to take the test.

You can also register on the *Jeopardy!* Web page:

http://www.spe.sony.com/tv/shows/jeopardy/

Another way to pretty well ensure a shot at the test is to go to Atlantic City and try out there. For two weeks a year, usually around February, *Jeopardy!* runs ongoing tryouts in Atlantic City at Merv Griffin's Resort Hotel Casino. Since thousands of people try out, there is a two-step process. First, you take a ten-question test on which you must get at least eight right to be called back to take the fifty-question test described in the next chapter. The great thing about trying out in Atlantic City is that you can take the ten-question quiz once a day, every day of the two weeks.

The problem with trying out in Los Angeles and Atlantic City is that *Jeopardy!* appears to take a much lower percentage of those who pass the test at these sites than of those who pass at contestant searches around the country. Of course, this is so *Jeopardy!* can have a geographically diverse contestant pool. I mean, how long would a fan who happens to be a librarian from Indiana care about *Jeopardy!* if all the contestants were attorneys from San Something, California?

Trying Out in Your Own Backyard

I personally was not willing to go out to L.A. just to take the test, so I had to come up with a way to determine when *Jeopardy!* was coming to my hometown or to a city nearby. Every year *Jeopardy!* travels around the country holding contestant searches in various cities. An announcement at the end of the *Jeopardy!* program in a given city will be aired about two weeks before the tryout date. It will inform you that *Jeopardy!* is coming to town and will tell you how you can be eligible. Usually, you send in postcards or call a local TV or radio station.

The problem is that you don't get much advance warning, and it's kind of hard to monitor the television programming in other cities. So I started scanning newspaper databases from previous years and found dozens of stories about *Jeopardy!*

contestant searches in various places. In fact, I learned that
Jeopardy! returns to certain cities frequently, often at the same
time each year. Below is a list of some of the places *Jeopardy!* has
gone to recently, along with information about how tryouts have
been conducted in each one. Of course, the specifics may change
from year to year.

JEOPARDY! TRYOUT LOCATIONS AND TIMES

Where	Time of Year	Local Contact	What You Had to Do
Seattle	Late June	WTEN Ch. 10	Send postcards to WTEN
Dallas	Early June	KSCS-FM 96.3	Call in radio station
Houston	Mid-June	KODA-FM 99.1	Win a call-in contest
Atlanta	Mid-May	WXIA-TV	Call 404-892-1611
Connecticut	May		Report to the Mohegan Sun casino in Uncasville, Connecticut, to take a 10-question test. Just as in Atlantic City, anyone can take the 10-question test. If you pass, you get to take a 50-question test later.
Boston	May or June	WHDH-TV	Send postcards to *Jeopardy!* or go to *Jeopardy!* Web page
Baltimore	March 31	WMAR-TV	Call TV station
Cleveland	Early May	WEWS-TV	Send postcards to WEWS
Sacramento	Mid-May	KXTV Ch. 10	Fill out a trivia contest found in *Sacramento Bee* newspaper

Jeopardy! seems to return to these locations often looking for contestants.

If you live in or near any of these cities, you should make sure to watch the show every day for three to four weeks before the relevant dates (like you wouldn't anyway). It is likely that *Jeopardy!* will come again. You also should call the stations in the cities close enough to drive to and simply ask them when the *Jeopardy!* tryouts are going to be and what you have to do to try out. The station to call is the one that airs the show. You may have to go to the library and look at the phone books for that city. Do not worry that you are sending postcards to a city in which you do not live. I'm sure they don't check the postmark when they get your postcards.

At the time I was making this list, I was in the first year of a two-year judicial clerkship with the Honorable Robert Krupansky in Cleveland and was planning to call everywhere from Memphis, Tennessee, to Windsor, Ontario, to find a nearby tryout. Then I came across some news stories about *Jeopardy!* coming to my own backyard, Cleveland, in prior years, usually in late March or early April. This was my chance.

Sure enough, one night in early April 1995, Alex's voice came on after Final *Jeopardy!* saying those magic words: "*Jeopardy!* is coming to your neck of the woods.... Send in a postcard to the address shown on the screen to be eligible for a tryout. Good luck." This was it! The show was coming right to me, and I was not going to miss this opportunity.

Go for It 100 Percent!

Now, you are about to get a little insight into the strategy of this book. If something's worth going for, it's worth going for 100 percent. So when I realized that I needed to get my postcard picked from among thousands, I went to my computer, and using WordPerfect, printed out 319 postcards. After buying close to sixty dollars' worth of stamps, I mailed the cards in from various mailboxes around the city, lest my postcards all hit the station at the same time. I mailed the postcards on the Friday a week and a day before the tryout. The station would call us some time the next week if we got picked, and the lucky ones would take the test on Saturday. (It's amazing how slow a week can be when you're waiting for a call.) Finally, on the Friday the day before the tryout, I got the call from the station. Along with 299 other hopefuls, I was to report the next day to the Holiday Inn for a tryout.

JEOPARDY! SECRET NO. **1**
You can send in more than one postcard when *Jeopardy!* comes to your city for a contestant search. I sent in 319.

At that point, I basically had one night to learn every fact on earth, which brings me to my first preparation tip: Don't let this happen to you! Be prepared. If you don't pass the test, you will not be on the show. It's that simple. So try to do the preparation chapters of this book before you even get a tryout.

But now, let's imagine that you've done just that. You are lean, mean, and stuffed to the gills with trivial knowledge. Your postcard has been picked and—you can hardly believe it— you're going to get a tryout. The next chapter tells you how to maximize your chances of passing the test and getting chosen for the show.

CHAPTER 2

Making the Cut

When my postcard got picked, I was so nervous I could hardly concentrate on anything for the rest of the day at work. I walked around in an excited haze, my mind awhirl with possibilities and decisions to make. Should I cram until late in the night, or should I get lots of sleep? What should I wear? Do I really want to go through with this thing?

Dress for Success

The first way to give yourself a leg up on the competition is choosing the right clothes to wear to the tryout. If you were producing *Jeopardy!*, who would you want on the show: the English teacher wearing a nice sweater and a well-made skirt, or the who-knows-what wearing the dirty jeans and the Molly Hatchet T-shirt that looks like it hasn't been taken off since the Rock Superbowl in 1985? (You might think I'm exaggerating, but I'm not. People dressed like that for the tryout.) Give the producers every reason to pick you and reject the others.

TIP FROM THE CHAMP   At the tryout, wear something nice that you might wear on the air. The coordinators will take a picture of you to show the producers of the program, so look good.

So show up in something that would be passable on the show itself. You probably want to wear something that you are comfortable in, but try to look like you expect to be on the show. I wore a suit, and the others who were picked from my tryout group wore suits, nice sweaters, skirts, neat buttoned-down shirts, and so on.

Okay, you've thrown on your lucky sweater and made it to the tryout location, which will usually be a hotel convention hall or local library. You will immediately see about three hundred people who look a little like you and appear to be just as nervous as you are. Which leads me to the first mistake you should avoid.

Don't Forget: First Impressions Count

As you wait to be let into the auditorium, you might be nervous and wondering where you stand in relation to the other hopefuls. You might be tempted to try to "psych out" your opponents, intimidate them, or brag on yourself to feel a little better about the whole thing. Whatever you do, though, stay on your best behavior, even when just in line waiting to get in.

I did not notice it at the time, but the *Jeopardy!* crew do not necessarily wear Jeopardy! uniforms. Thus, there's no way to know if the people milling around you are other hopefuls, *Jeopardy!* staff, or people from the local TV station. So do not be a jerk, because you do not know who is watching. A good rule of thumb is that if you mention your SAT score, your membership in Mensa, or your undefeated Trivial Pursuit record in the first ten minutes you are there, you might be perceived as a jerk.

Taking the Test

You will be required to show your identification, and then you will be given an answer sheet and a pencil and will be directed to find a seat in the auditorium. They will not yet tell you how they are going to administer the test, but it will probably be given via two TV monitors at the front of the auditorium. I recommend, therefore, that you sit up front, near the monitors. When all the seats are filled, a *Jeopardy!* spokesperson will come onstage, tell you one more time how hard it is to get on the show, slip in a few jokes, and then start the test.

There's good news and bad news about the *Jeopardy!* tryout test. The good news is that you do not have to answer in the form of a question. The answer sheet that *Jeopardy!* gives you has fifty short-answer blanks, and you just need to fill them all in. The bad news, especially for those who do not buy this book, is that the test is really hard. It is composed of only the $800 and $1,000 questions from the show, and you need to get thirty-five out of fifty right to pass. So study hard before you ever get to the tryouts.

JEOPARDY! SECRET NO. 2

- The *Jeopardy!* written test consists of 50 $800 to $1,000 questions from the show.
- You have to get 35 out of 50 to pass.
- You can try out every six months if you want.

As I mentioned, the test is usually given from a videotape via monitors located at the front of the auditorium. It contains fifty random *Jeopardy!* questions in fifty different categories. The questions will flash up on the screen and look just like they do at home, except that the category name will appear in the upper left-hand corner. Then Alex's voice will come on and read the

question. You will have approximately eight seconds to answer
the question before the next one starts.

Geography:

This South American city
got its name because it was
discovered by Portuguese
explorers in January

Sample question from qualifying
test. Did you know "What is Rio
de Janeiro?"

If You Don't Know, Guess

If you do not know the answer to the question right away, it is
important that you leave some kind of note to yourself on the
answer sheet to remind you what the question was about so that
you can go back and guess later. The videotape will not be
replayed, nor will you have any opportunity to ask the *Jeopardy!*
crew to explain or repeat any of the questions.

As much as you prepare, there is no way to avoid the fact that
a good amount of luck is involved in getting on the show. So
make sure that you at least put a guess down in every blank.
What you think is a dumb guess might just be the answer. Or,
who knows, maybe they will misread your handwriting and give
it to you anyway.

When I took the test in Cleveland in 1995, there were easily
twenty out of fifty questions that I either had no clue about or was
not sure of. I put down guesses on all of them, and some of those
guesses apparently were right because I passed. So always guess!

Also, when answering the questions, do not forget that
Jeopardy! often gives you more than one way to get the answer.
For example, you might know that "plié" is the answer to the
clue shown below because you are a ballet expert or because you
speak French. Additionally, if you try to recall all the dance-
related terms that you know and you remember the word plié,

you might notice it is similar to words like "pliant" or "pliable." That is what is so great about *Jeopardy!* questions: Different people can arrive at the answers in different ways.

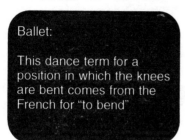

Ballet:

This dance term for a position in which the knees are bent comes from the French for "to bend"

There is more than one way to get "What is plié?"

If you cannot muster anything but the wildest guess on some of the questions, don't feel too bad, for you are not alone. One of the funniest things during the tryout is the groans, the shaking of heads, and the helpless chuckling when especially hard questions came up. During my tryout, there was one question about Alpine headgear that was so obscure that people started laughing out loud. Also, don't be surprised if, right around question 25, people start getting up and walking out. Trivial egos can be delicate, it seems.

However, I urge you not to join them. First, the monologue the spokesperson delivers while they are grading the tests is pretty funny. Second, you may amaze yourself by passing after all if you stick with it and luck out on some of your guesses—but you're sure to fail if you bail out. Third, many of the most successful champions in *Jeopardy!* history took the test many times before passing. Take Bob Scapose and Dave Sampugnaro, for example. Bob took the test over and over. Once he made it onto the show, he did all right: He was a semifinalist in the 1996 Tournament of Champions! Dave Sampugnaro is the poster boy for the benefits of perseverance. He took the test six times, passing twice, before he finally got on the show. All he did was win five games, $73,000, and the title of 1996's leading regular-season winner! So do not walk out. Hear as many questions as

you can and gain as much experience as possible. This may take
more than one shot.

You Passed! Now What?

When the test finally ends, the *Jeopardy!* crew will collect the
papers and take them out of the room for an excruciating ten
minutes of grading. During that time, everybody in the room
will, of course, discuss the questions and laugh about how
impossible they were. Everyone will seem to have known ten
more than you did, but don't worry, what matters is the official
test results. Finally, the staffers will return with a woefully thin
stack of the papers of those who passed. When I tried out in
Cleveland, only twenty-eight out of three hundred passed.

The *Jeopardy!* spokesperson will read off the names of those
who made it. When she or he gets to yours, I recommend
screaming, jumping up, and running to the front to kiss the host
as if you were on *The Price Is Right*. Actually, I'm just kidding.
Don't do that!

From this point on, the *Jeopardy!* crew is probably looking for
three things:

- Can you follow directions?
- Will you play the game with spirit?
- Will you freeze up in the interview?

If you scream and run up to the front after they have told you
not to come to the front until all the names are called, that is
sure to be a strike against you.

You and the others who passed will get a round of applause,
and the 90 percent who did not pass will get a nice consolation
speech and will be shown the door. Then you victorious ones will
file down to the front and begin filling out some paperwork.

There are lots of forms, including one that contains the five
anecdotes you want to discuss with Alex on the air. You should
have them prepared before you go to the tryout, because you are

kind of stuck with them from then on. Remember to follow directions when filling out the forms, and always be polite to the coordinators. (The forms might be lengthy and a little tedious, but do not complain about them. Your goal here is to be the "Stepford" contestant.) Then you are ready for the mock game and interview.

How'm I Doin', Coach?

Let me stop for a minute to tell you where you stand at this point. If you pass the test, your odds of making the show are suddenly pretty good, especially if you are taking the test in a remote market. Of the nine people in my mock-game group, seven appeared on the show, and two of us—schoolteacher Gordon Wean and I—made it to the Tournament of Champions. Good job, Cleveland!

From my experience at the tryouts, and from talking with other contestants, I believe that once you pass the test, you are assumed to be a viable contestant unless something tells them different. This could simply be that they already have too many dentists from Little Rock on the show, or it could be something about you—such as you are uncontrollably nervous, obnoxious, or simply incapable of following directions.

In other words, in the mock game and the interview segment of the tryout, you do not need to go out of your way to *prove* anything. You've already demonstrated that your brain is in shape. The best thing to do, therefore, is to relax and have fun from that point on. Do not try too hard to be witty, outgoing, or anything else. I mean, look at the people on the show: They're not exactly Jerry Seinfeld, are they? The last thing you want to do is come off as obnoxious.

The Mock Game and Interview

The contestant coordinators set up a rudimentary buzzer-and-light system on a table. You will be called up in groups of three to pretend to play the game itself. Each person will get an actual buzzer to hold, and the three of you will stand there just like on the show (but without podiums). Don't be surprised if your heart is pounding like it's the real thing, too. This is the first time you realize how brain-scrambling it is to stand up and answer trivia questions in front of people.

The questions for the mock game are written on posterboards stacked by category on the table. One coordinator will hold up a posterboard and start reading a question aloud. It's written on both sides of the posterboard so you can see it at the same time. As on the show, you have to wait until the end of the question to ring in. The buzzer setup they have is not quite like the one on the show, however, in that it does not lock anyone out (more on the show's buzzer later). Each person's light lights up whenever she presses the button even if someone else has already rung in. So the *Jeopardy!* folks can tell not only if you buzzed in but how; that is, whether you pressed it once or pressed it frenetically.

What They're Really Looking For No. 1: Following Directions

As I mentioned, at this point the *Jeopardy!* coordinators are looking at whether you can follow directions. They will tell you to press the button repeatedly every time you ring in, just as you should on the show. So do it! You will eventually get called on to answer, trust me. Also, the quickest way to mark yourself for rejection is to consistently fail to wait for the end of the question before ringing in. Again, this is a case of following directions.

Do not worry about how many questions you get right during the mock game—or how many you get wrong, for that matter. They don't care about numbers, because they already know you are smart enough to pass the dreaded qualifying test. If wrong answers killed your chances, I would not have been on the show. In fact, once I was *so* wrong that the coordinator paused, then said, "Huh?" and the room broke out in laughter. (The answer was "hormones," but I said "thermostat"—like I said, it scrambles your brain.) Also, I have talked to people who got lots of the questions right during the mock game and didn't make it, and to those who only got a few but were called. The unifying theme seems to be that those who follow directions and play the game with spirit are the ones more likely to get the call.

What They're Really Looking For No. 2: Playing With Spirit

What does it mean to play with spirit? Simple: Look like you're having fun up there. Smile, use a comfortable, reasonably loud voice, and do not whine or argue about the questions. Also, avoid pauses between the questions. One of the things the coordinators will tell you is to pick the next category *quickly* after you have answered a question. It looks much better on the air if you move right to the next category after answering, so do not wait for a prompt. This is something that I think is very important to the contestant selectors.

What They're Really Looking For No. 3: Will You Freeze Up in the Interview?

After everyone has rotated into the mock game and gotten a few questions, you will move to the interview segment. They set up a video camera (another reason to dress nicely) and ask you to speak for a minute or so. The idea is to see how you're likely to do during the interview segment with Alex. Just be relaxed, and don't worry if you're nervous. It's not like the contestants you see on the air are Cary Grant or anything.

Usually, the contestant coordinators ask interview questions like "What would you do if you won a ton of money on *Jeopardy!*?" Responses like "Well, maybe I'd finally get off welfare" or "I'd get me a bottle of booze, a broad, and a hotel room" will probably not get you on the show. The safest bet is travel, home renovation, or a new car. Stay away from the boring "invest it," which, although advisable from a financial stand-point, is not what America wants to hear. Also, don't try to be too clever or charitable. All you are trying to show is that you can talk even if you're nervous. Remember, you don't have to prove anything here.

Finally, just as your adrenaline is starting to crash, the tryouts will be over. The contestant coordinators will gather all the forms, take some Polaroids to attach to them, and send you, anticlimactically, on your way. In essence, they will tell you, "Don't call us, we'll call you." They might call tomorrow, they might call seven months from now, or they might never call you at all. And so the "Big Wait" begins.

CHAPTER 3

How to Prepare for *Jeopardy!*

So what do you do while you wait? The first step is to buy an answering machine if you don't already have one. Fortunately for you wannabe contestants, *Jeopardy!* will leave a message on your machine if they call and you are not home. They will *not* just move to the next person on the list. So you don't have to sit by the phone all day every day for months.

The next step is to prepare, prepare, prepare. Mastering the tryout, the buzzer, and betting is not going to matter much if you simply don't know the answers to the questions. What will you do, for example, if "Presidential Nicknames" comes up and the writers expect you to know "Old Hickory" from "Old Kinderhook"? I'll tell you what you'll do. You'll think back to this book, where you learned the 100 facts about presidents that are most likely to come up on *Jeopardy!*

Yes! You Can Prepare for *Jeopardy!*

This is the section where you learn how to prepare for the questions themselves. The question I am asked most frequently about *Jeopardy!* (after "What is Alex *really* like?") is whether the show gave us any idea about what the categories would be before we went out there. Some people speculate that they give us a huge notebook of questions to memorize or a list of categories that might appear. In reality, the answer is a resounding no. In fact, *Jeopardy!* goes to excruciating lengths to prevent even the possibility of the contestants knowing what will be on the show. After the game show scandals of the 1950s, the producers are understandably obsessed with secrecy. In short, contestants are told nothing about what questions will be on the show. Thus, the people you see up there every night really know all that stuff— and you can too!

But *Jeopardy!* asks about so many subjects, people say, that you cannot possibly study enough in a limited time to make a real difference. I am living proof that that simply is not the case. True, it would be a waste of time to try to memorize the entire World Almanac or Microsoft Encarta CD Encyclopedia. However, if you take the more selective and valuable approach shown in this book, you can dramatically increase your chances for *Jeopardy!* success.

JEOPARDY! SECRET NO. 3
Jeopardy! does not tell the contestants anything about what categories will appear or what questions will be on the show. In other words, the contestants really know all that stuff!

The Goal: Fifty Right Every Night

When I first began studying for the show, I averaged about forty right answers to the sixty-one questions *Jeopardy!* asked every night (i.e., thirty for Single Jeopardy!, thirty for Double Jeopardy!, and one Final Jeopardy!). I only got about half of the Daily Doubles and 40 percent of Final Jeopardy! questions right. By the time I was about to go on the Tournament of Champions, I got over fifty questions right every time and got four out of five Final Jeopardy! questions right every week. It was all because of proper preparation.

I admit that when I first began preparing for the show, I wasted a great deal of time finding the proper ways to study, and I read much useless information before I found things that improved my score every night. But this is good news for you. I have taken the time and done the research to determine the essential facts and techniques that you need to master to get at least fifty of the sixty-one questions right every time.

Proper preparation to win boils down to mastering four things:

- Evaluating your *Jeopardy!* strengths and weaknesses
- Learning to think like a *Jeopardy!* writer
- Adding the right kind of knowledge to your database
- Improving your recall speed

All of these steps are crucial; failing to take any one of them can be deadly. But if you meet all of these goals, you will be highly successful on *Jeopardy!*

That may not even be the most rewarding part of your *Jeopardy!* preparation. You will also find that you enjoy reading, going out to eat, traveling, watching TV, and going to movies much more than before once you have started immersing yourself in the world of *Jeopardy!* facts. As you move forward with your preparation, you will quickly learn that *Jeopardy!* truly does not deal in obscurities. Although the questions seem esoteric to the uninitiated, *Jeopardy!* really only asks about the most important concepts in each subject it covers. The problem for contestants is that *Jeopardy!* covers about forty thousand different fields of knowledge! So you should be learning a little bit about many things, without learning any in depth just yet.

Once you learn about things you otherwise never would have, every book you read or movie you see will be imbued with richer meaning as you pick up on more and more of the allusions and cross-references thrown in by the creator. Also, you will essentially be building up an index of the whole of human knowledge, and, when it's all over, you can go back and focus on some of the more fascinating topics you encountered. In any event, I hope that you will come to enjoy and appreciate more fully the staggering force of human ingenuity, creativity, and brilliance. If you do, you will truly be culturally literate.

Step One: Evaluating Your *Jeopardy!* Strengths and Weaknesses

The first step in any self-improvement scheme is to see where you need to improve. The only way to do this for *Jeopardy!* preparation is to watch the show and keep track of the categories you crush and those that crush you. So first of all, I recommend watching the show every night.

TIP FROM THE CHAMP Tape *Jeopardy!* every night and watch it using the PAUSE button as your buzzer. Only that way will you be able to practice giving answers under pressure.

I should point out right now that, as with most of the other preparation techniques in this book, to keep track of your statistics you need to record the show every night before you watch it. This allows you to pause the tape after every question and do some data crunching. As discussed below, it also allows you to practice using the buzzer and recalling facts. So I recommend that you go out and get a VCR if you do not have one and record the show every night.

The best way to capture your statistics is to make up two grids, six columns by five rows, one each for Single and Double Jeopardy! At the top of each column, you write a category (impossible to do if you do not have a VCR, by the way). Then, as the questions start flying, you mark in each of the cells whether you got the question right or wrong. If you got it wrong, you should also write a word or two to remind you later what the gist of the question was.

TIP FROM THE CHAMP   Make two 6 x 5 grids to keep track of how you do each night. Then you will know your weak categories. You may be surprised.

When the show is over, look back at your grids. Are there any categories in which you simply did not get any or got significantly less than in the others? When I encountered such a category, I went to the library and checked out a book or videotape on that subject. It was always the introductory book or one that dealt very generally with the topic.

Learn the Basics in Each Category

As I said before, *Jeopardy!* only asks about the basics in each category, so you can really increase your score just by reading introductory books in lots of categories. To find such books, begin by checking the listing in this book, on page 34. If you are still in college or about to enter it, try to take introductory courses in as many different areas as possible, especially music, art history, dance history, film, and other subjects that just do not come up in everyday life.

As time goes by, look back at the grids from previous weeks. Are patterns emerging? I found that I simply did not know common proverbs and sayings, perhaps because I lived in Japan from age three to age six and was not exposed to them. This hurt me in obvious categories, such as "Proverbs," but also on questions containing a pun. So I read and memorized the section of *The Dictionary of Cultural Literacy* covering proverbs and sayings and played the *Games Magazine* puzzles involving puns. I got a little better, but you know what they say: "You can't make a silk purse out of a sow's ear."

I also found that I was very weak in "International Cuisine," "Potent Potables," and questions about movies, though I did not think I would be. So I had no choice. I was forced to drink good wine, cook exotic foods, go to neat restaurants, and rent great movies. What a grueling study period that was. But somehow I got through it.

Some Categories Are Guaranteed to Come Up

You should be especially concerned with your prowess in certain categories. Perhaps still smarting from the comments of Maya Angelou, *Jeopardy!* included a category specifically dealing with cultural diversity in eight out of every ten games in the 1995–96 season. (Maya Angelou is a noted African-American poet, actress, *Sesame Street* regular, and singer. She complained, rightly, that there are not enough minorities represented as contestants on *Jeopardy!* and concluded, wrongly I think, that *Jeopardy!* somehow attempts to hinder minorities from getting onto the show.)

As an aside, it was my experience that *Jeopardy!* has exactly the opposite mind-set. The producers, in my opinion, are eager to have both the contestants and the questions represent as close to a cross-section of our society as possible. The problem is simply that the people trying out are still too many of the same white schoolteachers, writers, and lawyers that you always see on the show. At my tryout in Cleveland, for example, not a single person who would be identifiable on the show as African-American tried out, and eleven other contestants I spoke with could only recall at most one or two African-Americans at their tryouts. If this is true at all tryouts, then the percentage of African-Americans who try out and pass the test and then make it onto the show is really quite high.

In any event, *Jeopardy!* seems to include a specific culturally diverse category (in addition to an increased diversity in all their questions) in most of the games these days. Watch the show for a while and you'll see it's true: "Black Americans," "Hispanic America," "Women Writers," and similar categories appear over and over again, as they should, so you had better be strong in those categories. In part III of this book, I cover these topics in depth, and list several good quiz books on these subjects.

TIP FROM THE CHAMP At least once every week, *Jeopardy!* includes a specific culturally diverse category such as "Hispanic America" or "Black Writers." You should know these categories cold.

As you watch the show, you will begin to identify areas where you need to improve and will be ready to add knowledge in those categories. But before we turn to adding data to the database, let's talk about another way to get more questions right every night: learning how the question masters at *Jeopardy!* think.

Step Two: Learn to Think Like a *Jeopardy!* Writer

You have probably realized by now that *Jeopardy!* questions have a certain unmistakable style. The Emmy Awarders sure have noticed, awarding over a dozen Emmys to the *Jeopardy!* writing crew. One of the things that makes the questions so great is that many of them not only test your memory for facts but also require some puzzle solving. Another is that they usually offer more than one way to get to the answer. Sometimes it is a pun that could lead you to the answer, sometimes the questions in a particular column have a theme, and sometimes just knowing what the writers tend to ask about is enough to allow you an educated guess. Below are some techniques for getting inside the minds of the Emmy-winning *Jeopardy!* writers.

Jeopardy!'s Favorite Facts

Where the heck is the Gulf of Bothnia? Do you know? Well, *Jeopardy!* sure does. This fact came up three times in the 1995–96 season alone: in my fifth game (I got it), in the third game played by a champion from Saskatchewan (she got it), and

on a Daily Double that International Tournament champion
Michael Daunt faced in the semifinals of the Tournament of
Champions (he missed it).

The Gulf of Bothnia is the upward-sticking arm of the Baltic
Sea that separates Sweden and Finland. It is not the most
important body of water in the world, but it comes up as the
$800 or $1,000 question in "Bodies of Water" surprisingly often.
The same recidivism is true of "topaz." Not a "Gems and Jewels"
category can go by, it seems, without some reference to "this
golden gemstone." And if you get an American poetry question,
it will probably be about Robert Frost.

Yes, *Jeopardy!* has some favorite facts it asks about frequently.
Some have even achieved cult status. For example, if you ever get
a question about an indigenous population and that question
contains the phrase "Those Darn...," please say, "What are
Etruscans?" Why? Because "Those Darn Etruscans" is a famous
Jeopardy! category from the past which Alex and the question
writers still refer back to today. Knowing a little *Jeopardy!* history
can go a long way.

Watch for Easy Questions Disguised as Hard Ones

That category is also a classic example of one technique used by
the *Jeopardy!* writers. Sometimes they devilishly disguise easy
questions in hard wrapping, which makes the contestants seem
even more astounding than they already are. For example,
"Those Darn Etruscans" were a rather obscure indigenous
people who occupied the Italian peninsula before the Romans
took over everything. But when you see "The Etruscans established the city of Veii just north of the course of this river in
central Italy" on the *Jeopardy!* board, you are really seeing a
geography question about Italian rivers. Knowing that the Tiber
River is in central Italy is not nearly as impressive as memorizing
pre-Latin Italian history. But that is just what it looks like you
have done when you answer this question correctly on the show.

JEOPARDY! SECRET NO. 4

Jeopardy! loves to disguise easy questions as hard ones. Instead of asking, "What is the largest desert in Mongolia?" they will ask, "The Ulan Bator Railroad crosses this Asian Desert." When you answer, "What is the Gobi?" it looks like you've memorized Asian railroad routes, while you just know your deserts.

Another great disguised question was nailed by Ron Jin, my opponent in my first two games (we tied the first time around). Ron realized that when *Jeopardy!* asked about a city captured by the "Nawab of Bengal" in a certain year, they were really asking about the infamous "Black Hole of Calcutta" (an incident where 150 or so British soldiers were locked in a tiny cell), which is still tough but is considerably more well known than the dates and places of India's colonial wars. He answered with "Calcutta"— and he was right.

Don't forget: The questions at the top of the board are worth less, so they should be easier, and they are. If one of these seems too difficult, there is probably a way of getting the answer that you have not seen yet. Also, keep in mind that the answer to a $100 or $200 question is usually the "obvious" answer. Thus, when the $200 question in "The Bard" is "Shakespeare lived with a family in this capital city at the beginning of his career," the answer is the most obvious choice—London—because Shakespeare was, obviously, English. It does not matter that you never read about that period in the Bard's life; *Jeopardy!* is not expecting you to have. This one was a gimme.

JEOPARDY! SECRET NO. 5

Three unwritten rules of question writing:
- The question that they're really asking comes after the word "this" or "these."
- *Jeopardy!* never repeats an answer in a single category.
- The category in the rightmost column of the board often features wordplay or a hidden theme.

Unwritten Rules of Question Writing

I said before that knowing a little *Jeopardy!* history goes a long way. So does knowledge of some of the unpublished rules of question writing. Let's start with the basics.

Sometimes it's hard to figure out what the question is asking in the first place. A simple rule is that the "thing asked for" in each question comes after the word "this" or "these." For example, look at this somewhat confusing question: "Though it is reputedly associated with ESP, scientists say the purpose of this gland in the forehead has yet to be conclusively determined." Though the question talks about ESP and scientists, the real "thing asked for" is the name of a "gland" which is the word following "this" in the clue. The answer is pineal gland, therefore. So as you practice at home, watch out for the word "this" or "these" and realize that the next word determines the answer.

The second rule that can help you is that *Jeopardy!* never repeats an answer in the same column, even if the clues for that answer would be different each time. For example, imagine that the category is "Presidents" and the $100 clue is "This president and WWII general was once president of Columbia University." The response would be "Who is Eisenhower?" If the $300 clue is about a "Texan president," you know that it must be George Bush or Lyndon Johnson. It cannot be Eisenhower again. This can be very helpful when you have a question narrowed down to two or three possibilities.

Third, notice that several times a year *Jeopardy!* has a category in which all of the answers are linked by a hidden theme. Once, a category whose name did not refer to Elizabeth Taylor was nonetheless all about her. Another time, the $100, $200, $300, and $400 responses were club, heart, diamond, and spade respectively. The $500 clue was "All the clues above relate to these objects." That is one reason to pick from top to bottom, the producers will tell you.

JEOPARDY! SECRET NO. 6

Sometimes a category will have a theme, although the name does not suggest it. You should especially watch out for a hidden theme when picking the rightmost column of the board, which often has the "weird" categories in it.

By the way, did you ever realize that the arrangement of categories on the *Jeopardy!* board has a certain pattern? Crazy categories like the ones just described, as well as wordplay categories like "Crossword Clues," "C in Geography," "Anagrams," or— my favorite—"Puns," usually appear in the rightmost column. Light categories—about TV, music, toys, etc.—seem to fall on the left side of the board, with the hard stuff in the middle. Remember this when picking categories and coming up with guesses.

Watch, Play, Read

As you can see, the best way to learn to think like a *Jeopardy!* writer is to watch the show and think about the specific choices the writers made when they wrote the questions. You can do the same thing with the *Jeopardy!* home game. The questions are on convenient two-sided cards, and you should read all of them before you go on the show. Keep notes as you go on the categories you miss and focus on them later. The books written by Alex Trebek and *Jeopardy!* staff members are also useful, because they contain lots of questions written by the writers themselves. The facts in those questions come up again and again, though actual questions are never repeated. You should know every question in those books.

Perhaps the best way to think like a writer, though, is to go through the multiple-choice questions that come with the electronic hand-held game. If you go to any large toy or discount store and check the electronic game aisle, you will see that Tiger Electronics produces a hand-held game that allows you to pick the category, ring in, and keep score. Once you pick a category on the electronic device, it tells you where to look for the question in the booklet that comes with the game.

The booklet contains approximately 1,500 multiple-choice questions. Once you have used these up, you can purchase additional question booklets, and I urge you to buy all that you can find. Because all of the questions in them have actually been used on the show, they are a great clue to the *Jeopardy!* way of thinking.

The problem with these booklets is that they do not indicate the correct answer, so you usually have to play the electronic game to find it out. While it is fun to play with friends using the electronic device, waiting for the answer wastes time if you want to read many questions quickly to prepare for the show.

A better way to use the question booklets, I discovered, is to go through them one by one, without the electronic game. As you go, mark down the answers you know cold, but look up those you do not know immediately. When I was preparing for the Tournament of Champions, I spent an hour or two every day reading the question booklets at the computer. When I got to one I was not sure about, I would look it up on the Microsoft Encarta CD Encyclopedia. In researching the answer, I would invariably have to read all kinds of material in the same category. It might take awhile to plow through questions in this fashion, but this was extremely effective research time because it was about subjects in which I knew the *Jeopardy!* writers were known to be interested.

TIP FROM THE CHAMP   Buy the hand-held game and look up the answers to the multiple-choice questions in the question booklets. Doing the research will be more valuable than getting the answer.

Write Questions Yourself

Once you feel you are starting to think like a *Jeopardy!* writer, practice it. When you read the paper in the morning, or a book about jazz musicians, think about the questions you would write if you were a *Jeopardy!* writer. I even kept a notebook, which eventually turned into the collection of questions found in section III of this book. If you are close to another avid *Jeopardy!* fan, take turns writing *Jeopardy!* boards for each other. It will get you on the same wavelength as the writers and will be great fun to boot.

In short, the best way to learn to think like a *Jeopardy!* writer is to watch the show itself and to practice on any questions actually written by the *Jeopardy!* folks that you can get your hands on. Then practice that way of thinking whenever you can. Once you have determined what the *Jeopardy!* writers are looking for, you are ready to start adding the right kind of data to your trivia database.

Step Three: Adding the Right Kind of Knowledge to Your Database

Just by going through the multiple-choice questions in the hand-held game, you have already begun to learn a great deal of just the right kind of knowledge. But what if you have determined that you need to cover an entire subject—for example, ballet or American history? Below is a list of the most useful sources to start with.

General Knowledge

These are the books you will return to again and again as you prepare for the show. While it will not be possible to absorb all of the information in them, any time you spend reading these books will be rewarded. You can easily make flash cards for yourself, if the book isn't already organized as a handy study tool.

Dictionary of Cultural Literacy, E. D. Hirsch Jr., Joseph F. Kett, and James S. Trefil. Houghton Mifflin, 1988. ISBN: 0395655978.

Start here. Every single entry in this dictionary could be a *Jeopardy!* question. Co-author E. D. Hirsch thinks we all should know all this material and so does *Jeopardy!* Rely on this work repeatedly.

The New York Public Library Desk Reference. Paul Fargis and Sheree Bykofsky, eds. 2d ed. Prentice Hall General Reference, 1993. ISBN: 0671850148.

This work is very complete, so it has some information that is not going to come up. Its lists with brief information about authors, dancers and dancing terms, musicians and musical terms, mixed drinks, and a host of other topics make it invaluable.

The World Almanac and Book of Facts. Robert Famighetti, ed. Funk & Wagnalls, 1998. ISBN: 0886878217.

No surprise here, but pick this almanac over others for its lists of famous people with a little bit of information about each: Noted Writers, Noted Inventors, Noted Black Americans, Noted Scientists, etc. Almost all of them are likely to come up on the show.

1998 People Entertainment Almanac. Camille N. Cline. People Weekly, 1998. ISBN: 1883013208.

Jeopardy! always likes to throw in current entertainment questions, and this book is a virtual bible for that topic. From in-depth details of the Academy Awards to bestseller lists to plot summaries of the top operas, it has a ton of good material.

On the Tip of Your Tongue. Irene M. Francke. Signet, 1990. ISBN: 0451162811.

This powerful little book makes for very efficient learning. It sets out lists of thousands of facts, names, and concepts, organized by subject, with a short phrase that describes each one. "Egyptian leader who built the Aswan Dam" would be

Nasser. The book is divided into two columns; you cover the right side and quiz yourself using the phrases on the left.

An Incomplete Education. Judy Jones and William Wilson. Rev. ed. Ballantine, 1995. ISBN: 0345391373.

Not only a great way to get a smattering of knowledge about the academic stuff that comes up, but great fun to read.

Benét's Reader's Encyclopedia. William Rose Benét and Bruce Murphy, eds. New York: HarperCollins, 1996. ISBN: 006270110X.

Literature is one subject in which a little study can give you an immediate advantage over your opponents. This encyclopedia is a great place to look up Shakespeare, Dickens, Twain, Hemingway, Chaucer, and the other authors who come up over and over again.

The Bathroom Book, volumes 1–4. Steven Anderson, ed. Compact Classics, 1993. ISBN: 1880184109.

These clever little items condense the plots of famous books so you can read them in one "sitting." They also have trivia questions at the end.

Jeopardy! Books

These books are about the show itself. You should read all these if you can, especially the ones written by the *Jeopardy!* folks themselves.

The Jeopardy! Book: The Answers, the Questions, the Facts, and the Stories of the Greatest Game Show in History. Alex Trebek and Peter Barsocchini. ISBN: 0060965118.

This title is out of print. Although it is no longer available from the publisher, you can obtain it using Amazon.com. This is the original authorized behind-the-scenes account and the place to start to learn about the show. It's also packed with questions.

The Jeopardy! Challenge: The Toughest Games From America's Great-

est Quiz Show. Alex Trebek and Merv Griffin. ISBN:
1559946636.
> This title is out of print. Although it is no longer available
> from the publisher, you can obtain it using Amazon.com. It's
> well written, includes plenty of sample questions, and gives
> some nice behind-the-scenes anecdotes—but nothing too
> juicy.

Inside Jeopardy!: What Really Goes On at TV's Top Quiz Show. Harry
Eisenberg. James Van Treese, ed. ISBN: 156901177X.
> Harry Eisenberg, former *Jeopardy!* producer, wrote this con-
> troversial and very revealing exposé after he left the show.
> According to newspaper accounts, *Jeopardy!* personnel were
> very upset about some of his allegations, particularly that
> categories were picked for the tournaments in order to favor
> women contestants. Eventually, this book was pulled out of
> stores and replaced by a more conservative version, listed
> next.

*Jeopardy!: A Revealing Look Inside TV's Top Quiz Show: Contestants
and Question Selection Process Unveiled.* Harry Eisenberg. Lifetime
Books, 1997. ISBN: 0811908615.
> This version of Eisenberg's book was supported by the
> *Jeopardy!* powers-that-be.

Secrets of the Jeopardy! *Champions.* Chuck Forrest and Mark
Lowenthal. ISBN 0446393525.
> Written by two former champions, this out-of-print book is
> full of facts in the classic *Jeopardy!* categories but is a little light
> in the strategy department, probably because Mr. Forrest was
> so brilliant that he did not need to use much strategy to crush
> his opponents. You should try the library to find this valuable
> book.

Step Four: Improving Your Recall Speed

One of the things that amazes people about *Jeopardy!* contestants
is the speed at which they can recall all that trivia. Actually,

though, I should let you in on another *Jeopardy!* secret. The time that the contestants in the studio have to answer each question after it is revealed is about five seconds longer than it looks when you watch it at home. There are several reasons for this. First, the question is visible to the contestants in the studio as soon as it is uncovered, while at home the question starts out as a small dot on the TV screen and then enlarges to fit the full screen. Second, when the question appears in the studio, Alex takes a second or two to scan the question before he begins reading it. During this time, the contestants can read the question as well. The technicians apparently edit out this delay when the show is put together. Third, when you are watching at home, the camera cuts right to the contestants as soon as Alex finishes the question. In the studio, the question is still on the playing board, so the contestants can still see it. More than once, I rang in with one answer in mind and then changed my mind after reading the question again. Thus, you do not have to be as fast as the contestants seem on the air, but you still need to be pretty quick at recalling things.

JEOPARDY! SECRET NO. 7
Contestants in the studio have about five seconds longer to answer the question than it appears at home.

Study Actively, Not Passively

Can you really improve your recall speed? The answer is definitely yes, but you have to work at it. Like anything else in the body, if you practice using your memory, it will get better—and it will do so very quickly. But you have to force yourself to study actively, not passively. This involves two things: active question answering and rote memorization.

By "active question answering," I mean that just reading questions and answers every day is not enough. You must read each question, say your answer to yourself or a partner, and only then check the answer. Actually saying the answer seems to be important in increasing recall speed. If you find yourself just reading the questions and answers without trying to come up with the answer every time, stop. If you just want to read passively, your time will be better spent turning to an introductory text in one of your weak areas. You can learn new material passively, but to improve recall speed you must focus on the specific task of recalling and stating information.

The second technique for improving recall speed is rote memorization. When you are trying to memorize every fact on earth, you learn a great deal about your memory. In fact, during my *Jeopardy!* preparation, I made a strange discovery. If I memorized and went over flash cards about U.S. presidents, for example, later I could better remember the names of famous paintings—without ever studying the paintings. Even more surprising, if I went over flash cards and then did a crossword puzzle, I could complete it much faster than if I did not go over flash cards first. Even more surprising than that, after I went over flash cards every day for a month, my speed at seemingly unrelated mental tasks stayed at higher than normal levels all day.

This was hardly a scientific study, but it seemed that rote memorization and quizzing were like calisthenics for the brain. You improve your mental ability across the board by doing them every day. Thus, I recommend that you memorize a list of things (badge numbers of the people in your Kiwanis Club, capitals of South American countries, current averages of the Boston Red Sox starting nine...it doesn't matter what) every day, even if you are never planning to go on a quiz show. Your overall mental performance will soar as if you have taken some intelligence-increasing drug, trust me. So rote memorization every day is important not so much for the facts you will learn but for the increase in mental speed and recall ability it will provide you.

Putting It All Together: A Sample Day

Every day, you should work on each of the four steps in proper preparation. During the seven months after my tryout but before I got "the call," I used the following study regimen. First, after getting ready for work, I would read *USA Today* and the local paper cover-to-cover, jotting down any potential question ideas, especially Final *Jeopardy!* questions. There may be better papers out there than *USA Today*, but not for *Jeopardy!* preparation. Then, before going out the door, I would set the VCR to record *Jeopardy!* that night. On the way to work, at lunch, or on the way home, I would memorize some list, such as world capitals, presidents and their vice presidents, etc., just to keep my mind going at super speed all day. Then I would take a break from it until after my daughter was asleep that night.

THINGS TO DO DAILY
- Read the paper
- Record the show
- Memorize something
- Have someone quiz you for an hour
- Watch the show as if it's a workout
- Review your stats
- Read an introductory text

After my daughter was asleep, my wife would quiz me for about an hour from the sources listed above, and then I was ready for my *Jeopardy!* workout for the day.

The Show as a "Trivia Workout"

To get the most out of the show itself, I recommend simulating stage conditions as much as you can. Set up a makeshift podium in front of the TV. The podium should be the same height as the one on the show, and you should stand while practicing. The podium should have a place to rest your buzzer hand, and there must also be enough room for you to write on a piece of paper.

Make game grids to keep track of the questions you get right and get wrong. (See page 24, where I describe these grids.)

Then pop in the tape with the day's *Jeopardy!* episode on it. Using the PAUSE button on the remote control, stop the tape and fill out the categories on your grid. Now you are ready to go.

Holding the remote control in your hand with your thumb on the PAUSE button, pretend it is your buzzer and play along at home. You should practice waiting for Alex to finish reading the question before pressing PAUSE. If your timing is right, by the time the VCR pauses, the camera will have cut to the players and one player's light will just be turning on. If you press PAUSE and the question is still on the screen, you are probably "ringing in" too early. If the player's light has been on awhile, you are too late. See chapter 5 for more information.

Once you ring in by pressing the PAUSE button, practice saying the answer and then picking the next category. Do not just think the answer; actually say it. You will then realize how brain-scrambling it is to keep track of the question, Alex's voice, the buzzer, the answer, and the next category. But the more you practice it at home, the easier it gets.

I will talk about this more in a later chapter, but make sure you also practice taking a second to think before you give your answer. You will prevent many a dumb error, and you will feel generally more in control, if you are in the habit of thinking through every question before delivering an answer. You have five seconds to say your answer once you ring in, so do not be afraid to use all of your time.

Once you pretend to pick the next category, un-pause the tape to see if you got the question right. If you did, try to put a check in the box on the grid without pausing the tape. This will practice your ability to concentrate on the game while other distractions are going on. If you got it wrong, pause the tape again and write a word or two reminding you what the question was about, to use later when evaluating your strengths and weaknesses. This all will seem incredibly distracting at the beginning, but it will make the studio experience seem like a breeze in comparison. Well, maybe not a breeze, but definitely easier.

Eventually, one of the players is going to get a Daily Double. When it happens, pause the tape, give yourself an imaginary score, and practice coming up with a bet. Sometimes people on the show seem never to have thought about how to bet if they get a Daily Double. Do not let that happen to you. By the time you get to the sound stage, you should have placed hundreds of Daily Double bets. In chapter 6, I lay out some of the strategies in betting on Daily Doubles; you should be very familiar with them all, because they can really turn a game around. When Final Jeopardy! comes around practice actually making a bet (again, see chapter 6) and writing your response down in the time allotted. It will make a difference later, trust me.

Once you finish the mock game, your adrenaline will probably be flowing. To fall asleep, I usually had to read something, so I picked the introductory text in one of my weaker areas. Though I simply read through these books without really studying them, I learned a great deal just from osmosis. A fair amount of that information came up on the show.

If you follow the regimen given above, I guarantee your performance on the show will get significantly better. Keep track of your progress as time goes by, and you will see your scores soar. To beat your opponents on the show, you need to be able to get over fifty of the sixty-one questions right each night when no one is playing against you. That should be your goal: to get fifty out of sixty-one right every night by the time you get "the Call." You can do it!

The next chapter is all about what happens once you get "the Call." It takes you into the greenroom and right onstage to slug it out with America's brightest. Let's go for it!

CHAPTER 4

You Got the Call!

I warn you now: you will get your call from the *Jeopardy!* people when you are least prepared and when being on the show is about the furthest thing from your mind. I do not know why this is true, but it seems to be a basic law of the universe. I was in Cleveland, seven months after I tried out, when they called me. At the time, I had a million things on my mind. My daughter was changing preschools, my wife was starting a new job, and the holidays and lots of traveling were coming up. Maybe it was a good thing that *Jeopardy!* had not called yet, I thought. But as soon as I had that thought, it seemed, the phone rang. The voice on the phone said, "Hi! Mike, Glenn Kagan from *Jeopardy!* here. This is the call you've been waiting for!" He congratulated me on being picked and told me that I was to report to *Jeopardy!* a month later, ready to play. They would send out some details by mail, he said, and that was it—I was going to be on the show! After my wife and I jumped around the living room for a while and called a dozen or so people, we began to plan.

Getting Yourself Together

For the next month, I altered my preparation techniques slightly, focusing on increasing recall speed and trying to think like the writers rather than on trying to learn new material. Also, every day, I worked more and more questions trying to build up my stamina. For I knew that once I got out there, I might have to play five games of *Jeopardy!* right in a row.

Five Shows, Five Outfits

"Why five games?" you may ask. Many people think that a five-day champ spends a week out in Los Angeles taping the five episodes, filming one each day and sightseeing the rest of the time. And you have probably noticed that the champion wears a different outfit every show, so your assumption seems to be true. In reality, though, that would not be a very efficient way to run a game show. Instead, *Jeopardy!* tapes five shows a day every Tuesday and Wednesday. Thus, they complete two full weeks of airplay in two days. They go to great lengths, however, to preserve the illusion that the champion is actually out there all week.

JEOPARDY! SECRET NO. **8**
Jeopardy! tapes five shows a day, two days a week. The returning champion has to run back to the greenroom to change between games.

This means several things to you as a competitor. First, when you get to the *Jeopardy!* studio, you need to have five different outfits with you. You will have to run back to the greenroom to change your clothes in the fifteen minutes between games, so make sure you are organized. Second, you might be playing *Jeopardy!* all day, so you had better work on extending your ability to keep your concentration over time. Third, to be able to whip through five shows a day, *Jeopardy!* assembles all of the contestants who will appear in those shows at the beginning of the day. So expect to spend a great deal of time in the "greenroom" with the other contestants who may get a chance to play that day, waiting your turn.

But I'm getting ahead of myself; first you need to get out there. Here's another secret many people do not know about the show. *Jeopardy!* does not pay for anything when you go out there during the regular season. You have to pay for your own flight, hotel room, meals, and rental cars. Only if you make it to the Tournament of Champions do they pay for your flight and hotel. So round up the money somewhere, make the reservations, and pick out the clothes you need to pack.

What Looks Good on TV

Pure white shirts, white dresses with busy patterns, and suits or ties with small stripes or tight patterns look different on the show than they do at home. White is so bright that it bleeds over, and small stripes or tight patterns show up much more dominantly on camera than in person. All-black suits also seem to throw off the color balancer in the camera and look strange at home. So I recommend avoiding those colors and patterns. The best bets are medium-hued jackets, pastel-colored shirts, and solid ties for men, and solid-colored dresses or pantsuits for women. Also, the *Jeopardy!* people take care of last-minute makeup, but women should apply their usual makeup before coming to the studio.

Avoid Disaster: Carry on Your Five Outfits

If you're going to fly to California please heed this warning: Carry your five outfits on the plane with you. Do not check them with your luggage.

Why do I consider this so important? Let me tell you a personal nightmare-come-true.

When it was finally time to fly out to California, I felt ready. My bags had been packed the night before with my five best outfits. I had picked out a few particularly useful books for some last minute cramming on the flight, and those were neatly arranged in my carry-on case. I even got to the Delta Airlines terminal well before my flight was due to leave. I checked my three bags and went to the gate. Everything was going like clockwork.

As I jetted my way across two time zones, I was surprised by my composure. I calmly reviewed some material, did a few puzzles, and just relaxed. When I arrived in Los Angeles after an uneventful flight, it was 10:55 P.M. local time (it was 1:55 in the morning back home in Cleveland). I collected my carry-on items and calmly went down to the baggage collection area to grab my stuff and get to the hotel.

I am happy to report that my airline successfully delivered 67 percent of my luggage—a fine average in the major leagues, I suppose, but just not satisfactory to me at the moment. For, you see, the bag that they left behind was the one holding my five outfits to wear on the air. After the last, lonely pieces of luggage from my flight had circled the conveyor belt and left with their happy owners, I began to realize that no more garment bags would be coming out of the little door I had been staring at for half an hour. By this point, it was 11:30 P.M., in a city I had never been to before. Approximately ten hours later I had to be in the studio to fulfill my lifelong dream—and I had no suits.

Nervous breakdowns can be quite beneficial if timed properly. I was getting pretty worried now, and I looked around and noticed an office that had BAGGAGE CONTROL CENTER (or some similarly oxymoronic title) on the door. Ignoring the sudden wobble in my legs, the mild trembling in my hands, and the dryness of my throat, I went in hoping for the best.

Let me say right now that the people in that room have the worst job in the world. Their only customers are people who just had the bottoms drop out of their worlds. For example, the person before me in line was a German poet who had lost a manuscript he had worked on for over a year. After I heard that, my suit problem seemed pretty insignificant.

When I got to the counter, I immediately saw just why they lost people's luggage. The entire countertop was covered with small, random slips of paper, each containing some apparently crucial bit of information. I told them my flight number and what I was missing, and they searched through these scraps and through computer files trying to figure out what was going on. At first, they insisted that my garment bag had actually been delivered and that I had simply missed it.

Then, one of the scraps of paper caught my eye. I pulled it out of the pile and asked, "Could this mean anything?" It said the following:

Dupee—Ex 24
Cincinnati
FL1425 11A

The head attendant read it and said, "Oh, no problem, we left your bag in Cincinnati, but it will be sent at eleven o'clock. It should be here any minute." Then I asked—although I did not want to—"What does the little *A* mean right there?" She started to answer, stopped, started again, and then replied, "Oh, that means eleven A.M., tomorrow."

My heart dropped, a lump formed in my throat, and my eyes started burning as if I were about to cry. It was pushing midnight in L.A. at this point, and my options were dwindling fast. I made them check on the computer for every flight leaving any airport within driving distance of Cincinnati. I even went behind the counter and watched to make sure they were hitting the right buttons. Nothing worked. There simply was no way to get my bag to L.A. before eleven tomorrow morning. I needed to be in the studio, with my suits, by ten o'clock.

I left the airport feeling like I had been mugged. I hurried over to the car rental agency, and as I got the car I told them my story. They were horrified and were very nice to me. The manager let me borrow one of the Budget Rent-a-Car jackets and one tie. So I now had a pair of black dress pants, brown topsiders, a blue blazer, a white shirt, and an orange-and-blue tie to wear. None of it matched. Hey, at least I had something for one show.

But I planned to win five games, of course, so I needed more outfits. I went to a phone booth and checked the yellow pages for department stores that would be open late or early. All the mall stores, TJ Maxx's, and Ross Dress for Less wouldn't open until ten, and nothing in the vicinity was open twenty-four hours. The only store that would be open early, at eight A.M., was Target. I jotted down the location of a nearby Target and rushed to the hotel to get some sleep.

It was not to be a restful night, however. My mind was whirling a million miles a minute, and my stomach thought I had swallowed a hyperactive Slinky. I was so paranoid about missing my alarm that I woke up in a panic every time I did manage to doze off. I don't think I slept more than twenty minutes in a row that night.

Eventually the morning came, and I ran out to Target at 7:30 A.M., a half-hour before it opened. Now, I remember having a great time as a teenager camping out for concert tickets, but I never thought that I would have the experience of camping outside a Target so that I could get in right when it opened to buy clothes. It was a rather strange feeling, but I was not alone. Several blue-haired ladies were waiting with me, coupons in hand, ready to go. When I told them my story, they took me under their matronly wings and were determined to help me get what I needed.

We realized rather quickly, however, that Target simply did not carry suits. This was a problem, but not an insurmountable one. I had seen men on the show with just sweaters and ties, so I picked out four sweaters and four ties. The ladies also found one pair of pants that came with a matching jacket and were close to my size. The problem was that they were a hideous mix of khaki, olive green, and chartreuse; I was lucky that Danny Terio of *Dance Fever* had not seen them first, because he would have snatched them right up. To give you an idea of how awful this suit was, keep in mind that the entire thing—jacket and pants—cost $29.99.

But by this point, appearance really did not matter. I just wanted to be able to walk onto that stage in something. So I thanked my new fairy godmothers, got my sweaters, my oddly colored suit, my ties, and a garment bag (so I would not look different from the other contestants), and headed to the studio. Breakfast? Sleep? Who needs 'em!

Behind the Scenes at the *Jeopardy!* Studio

In the packet of information they send you, *Jeopardy!* will tell you to come to the Sony Pictures Studios in Culver City, California, for two days, usually a Tuesday and a Wednesday. They shoot five shows each day. *Jeopardy!* invites thirteen contestants each day because to tape those five shows they need at least eleven people (two new contestants each game, plus a returning champion) and they want to make sure they have enough people in case someone passes out or something (it has happened, according to the contestant supervisors).

An Awe-Filled Arrival

When I arrived at the studio that Tuesday morning, I quickly forgot about my lost-luggage fiasco. I was too excited. The guard at a security kiosk at the entrance of the parking lot told me where to park and directed me to wait at "the *Jeopardy!* Contestant Waiting Area," which was simply a little bench where the *Jeopardy!* contestants congregate before being taken to the studio. A small tram would come by a few minutes later to pick us up, he said.

As I tried to find the bench, I just soaked in the surroundings. The Sony Pictures Studios are amazing. You enter through a huge arch on which a beautiful mural is painted, just like it is on the opening credits of the show. When you go in, you immediately see massive sound stages all around you, which make the place look just the way you would imagine a Hollywood studio should look. The reserved parking lots behind the sound stages are filled with more Jaguars, Porsches, and BMWs than I ever expected to see in one place. I kept my eyes peeled, hoping to see stars pop out of doors at any time.

But I also was wondering what to expect. Would the other contestants be cutthroats, trying to psych each other—and me— out all the time? Or would they be nice but nervous? Would the contestant coordinators just throw us up onstage without any practice? Was this going to be fun or just nerve-wracking?

Meeting the Competition: A Pleasant Surprise

I turned a corner and saw a bench filled with people obviously waiting for a tram. My spirits lifted immediately. They were dressed nicely but casually and were chatting, laughing, and having a great time. "Wow, these people are really friendly," I thought. "This is going to be a blast." So I smiled and walked up to the group. About a step away from them, however, I saw the sign: WHEEL OF FORTUNE CONTESTANT WAITING AREA. Then I looked up. About fifty yards farther along was another bench. Several very nervous-looking people wearing dark suits were sitting there, not really talking to each other; more than one was poring over a book. I immediately knew what show they were waiting for.

But when I got there, they turned out to be just as friendly, though definitely more subdued. In fact, once all the contestants arrived I was very pleasantly surprised that there was not a jerk among us. By the time Glenn Kagan arrived to take us to the sound stage, we were all laughing together like old friends.

In the Mysterious "Greenroom"

When you get to the room where the contestants hang out between shows (the "greenroom," they call it in show business), you will begin to get a sense of the security they have on the show. Because of the game show scandals of the 1950s, as

portrayed in the movie *Quiz Show, Jeopardy!* keeps a very close
eye on its contestants. Thus, once you get on that tram, you are
treated almost like a member of a sequestered jury. You cannot
go anywhere on the set without a contestant coordinator along,
including the bathroom. If you are still around for the lunch
meal, you have to eat it with the rest of the contestants in a
separate corner of the studio commissary. The coordinators
basically want to avoid any possible appearance that you have
talked to the writers or producers of the show before going on.

JEOPARDY! SECRET NO. **9**
Jeopardy! is incredibly concerned with security. While you are a
contestant you cannot go anywhere on the set unescorted. This is
to avoid any appearance of cheating like that in the movie *Quiz
Show*.

In the greenroom, the first thing you will do is fill out lots of
forms. (Actually, the first thing I did was eat a bagel. As I said, I
had missed breakfast. Luckily for me, the greenroom is stocked
with all kinds of doughnuts, fruit, bagels, and drinks.) In the
forms you sign, you make many promises: You are not related to
Merv Griffin; you do not work for Sony Pictures; you will not
mention somebody's name or business on the air for compensa-
tion; you will not reveal the outcome of any game until it airs;
etc.

One interesting provision of the rather lengthy contract
allows you to pick a charity to which your winnings in excess of
$200,000 will go. (It used to be only $100,000, but because they
now give a car to five-time winners, they raised the limit.) I hope
that this provision applies to you when you go on the show!

After the forms are filled out, Suzanne Thurber, the head
contestant coordinator, will give everyone a nice pep talk. You
should be proud just to be on the show, she will tell you, even if
you come in third when you are up there. Of the thirteen people
in the room, only five at most could be winners today. The rest

will go home having lost on the show but having had a great experience. And people will be very impressed just that you were on the show, she promises, regardless of your success.

As you can see, the contestant coordinators are very supportive and very nice. After the pep talk, Suzanne and Glenn Kagan discussed how to play the game and even gave out strategy tips on picking categories, using the buzzer, and Final Jeopardy! betting. Then another *Jeopardy!* staff member came by and refreshed our memory about the anecdotes we planned to discuss with Alex on the air. It was a neat way to get to know about the other people in the room, as you listened to their anecdotes ahead of time. After that was over, we all chatted for a few minutes, until a staffer announced that we were ready to go onto the sound stage to get some practice.

Wow! A Quick Tour of the Amazing Sound Stage

Walking onto the sound stage for the first time was one of the coolest experiences of my life. What we see at home hardly captures the technological wizardry and elegance of the set that you see in person. The playing board is easily fifteen feet high, with thirty-six TV monitors in it—each at least thirty-one-inch screens, I guessed. At the edges of the set, off camera, two huge televisions are mounted in the wood paneling to show the questions to those in the audience.

A large camera, used to film Alex and the questions as they appear on the playing board, is right in the middle of the studio. It can be moved back and forth, or lowered and raised, with a single joystick. Its controller sits in a chair that is part of the camera assembly. The other camera, which shoots the players, is discreetly hidden in a small gap in the paneling to the left of the playing board. You do not really notice it while playing, although you can see the red light on top when it is on the air.

Also to the left of the playing board, and up high, are the "tote boards." These display the scores of the contestants and look just like the displays at the front of the podiums. So if you see the contestants glancing up at times while they are playing, they are probably checking their scores.

JEOPARDY! SECRET NO. 10
Have you ever wondered how the players know their scores without looking at the front of their podiums? The players can read their scores by looking up and to their left at big tote boards. That's why you sometimes see players looking in that direction, especially when placing Daily Double bets.

The spectator area is surprisingly small, seating only a couple of hundred people. They use canned conversation for the talking that you hear at the beginning of the show and canned applause if the crowd is not loud enough. When I was there, though, a school group was in (which Alex loved), and they were quite enthusiastic. No dubbing was needed that day.

At a table in front of the crowd, on the left side if you're facing the stage, sit the mysterious judges. You may see Alex look to his right at times when he is not sure whether an answer is acceptable. He is looking over at the judges, who check some thick book on their table or get on the telephone that is also on their table. I don't know much more about them, however, because we simply were not allowed anywhere near them.

I did notice that there are two technical assistants to the left of the judges. One of them uses a computer monitor and a light pen to pick the next category and to add or subtract from the players' scores. The monitor is pretty cool; it looks a lot like the *Jeopardy!* computer game. The other assistant is the all-important buzzer person. You cannot see this person when you are onstage, but he is the one responsible for determining when Alex finishes the question and when the players can ring in, which I talk about more in chapter 5. He is holding a small box attached by a wire to the table. On the box is a button, which he presses when he thinks that Alex is done. This motion is imperceptible from the podiums, so do not even bother looking.

Stepping Up to the Podiums

After we ogled the gorgeous set for a few minutes, the stage manager, John Lauderdale, led us over to the podiums. They were simply technological marvels.

From the front, they look sleek and almost simple. But from the back, you get an idea of their complexity. On the top, facing you, you find two small white lights that go on if you are the one who rings in first. In front of them are a row of ten red lights that indicate how much time you have left to answer once you have rung in. They are all lit when you ring in, and they go out one on each side as your five seconds tick off. A diffuse light rests on the podium aimed up at the contestants. It is used during Final Jeopardy! to light up only the contestants' faces, to give them that thoughtful look.

In the middle of the flat part of the podium is the area where the contestant writes the Final Jeopardy! wager and response. It looks like the screen of a laptop computer, and you write on it by using a special light pen that is attached to the podium. It is pretty hard to use, and that is why the contestant's handwriting sometimes looks bizarre.

Finally, in a holder attached to the side of the podium is the dreaded buzzer. About an inch wide and four inches long, the buzzer is attached by a long, flexible wire to a computer inside your podium. (The lower part of the podium is not very glamorous. It looks like the back of your entertainment center, with all kinds of wires and plugs everywhere.) In the middle of the top of the buzzer is a small, springy button that you will be pressing very frequently very soon. After stage manager John Lauderdale finishes his instructions, you are ready for the practice game.

Yes, You Get to Practice First

That's right, you get to practice under actual game conditions before you go out there in front of the cameras. The coordinators will pick three people at random, and the rest will sit nearby.

The chosen three will line up offstage, just as the contestants will before the actual game. Johnny Gilbert will be there and will practice reading out their names as they march out to the podiums. Glenn Kagan will then appear, filling in for Alex. He will give a funny little monologue, and then the game will start. These players will play for a while, and then the coordinators will begin rotating people in.

SNEAKY TIP FROM THE CHAMP   When the contestant coordinators take you out to the sound stage and over to the podiums, step right up to one of the podiums that is not the champion's. The stage manager, John Lauderdale, will eventually come over and instruct the contestants about how to write their names, how to talk in to the microphone, and how to use the buzzer. If you are the one who just "happens" to be at the podium when he starts, he will use you as an example, and you will get 10–15 extra minutes' practice with the buzzer.

You should play the practice game as though it were the real thing, except you should try getting in on every question even if you do not know the answer. The idea is to get used to the buzzer; if you don't know correct thing to say, just say something really silly. I offer one caveat, however. The technical assistant who determines when Glenn finishes the question and activates the buzzers is not the same person who does it during the show, and Glenn obviously reads with a different rhythm than Alex does. So the timing will be different in the real thing. (See chapter 5 for more buzzer tips.) In fact, it was my experience that you needed to press the buzzer sooner after Alex finished the questions than you did when Glenn was reading them in the practice game.

My First Day in the Greenroom

After everyone gets a chance to practice at the podiums, you will all go back to the greenroom to await the selection of the first contestants. Since *Jeopardy!* has no idea who will win each game, they cannot tell you ahead of time in which game you will appear or when it will air. Instead, the contestant coordinators announce the people who will be playing in the next game only five minutes before the game starts.

It will be nerve-wracking, and conversation will subside as you wait. The returning champion, if there is one, will be doing his or her final preparations, and everyone else will watch the door. One contestant likened it to his days working in a factory, waiting for the foreman to come down with the pink slips. It was pretty tense.

At that point in my *Jeopardy!* experience, I was beginning to come down from my adrenaline rush, and my tiredness began to kick in. I did not feel sharp but decided that I wanted to be picked first, while I had some energy left. That did not happen. The contestant coordinators soon came in and picked two other people to play against the returning champ. The rest of us were led out to a segregated portion of the audience area to watch the game.

One of the contestants that first game was Dave Sampugnaro, who when I met him in the greenroom seemed about the most nervous member of our little group. But when he got onstage he was a one-man wrecking crew, especially on the Daily Doubles. He hung with the champion and beat him by getting the Final Jeopardy! answer.

After each game, the losers are shown the door, and the champion goes back to the greenroom to change outfits. The contestant coordinators then come over to the segregated portion of the audience where the contestants are sitting and announce the names of the next two contestants. The two new contestants get to return to the greenroom for about fifteen minutes to freshen up. The other contestants remain in the audience.

When the coordinators came over and announced the contestants for the second game that day, they again did not pick me. By the time that game was over, I was definitely feeling tired, and Dave Sampugnaro was just getting stronger. I really did not want to play him, and I was happy that I did not get picked for the third game that day, either. Dave won the third game handily (Alex commented before Final Jeopardy! that the other players' scores "paled" in comparison), and we were ready for lunch. You will be happy to hear that if you survive past the third game, they will buy you lunch.

At this point, only seven people returned to the greenroom; Dave had already sent six people home. I really did not want to be his next victim. When the coordinators came in and announced that two people other than me would play Dave in the fourth game, I heaved a sigh of relief. Could I possibly make it through the day without having to face Dave—and without having to appear on TV in my hastily purchased sweater and tie?

I did not think it was possible, but Dave played even better in the fourth game, against tough competition. In a few moments, the coordinators came over with the names of the two people who would have to play next. At that point, four contestants remained. Two of us would have to play a four-time champ who was just getting stronger, and two of us would get to come back the next day and not have to face a returning champion at all. For me it was just like first-year law school all over again: "Don't pick me. Please don't pick me." They did not pick me. A philosophy professor from Texas and I got to come back the next day.

From that point on, everything went right for me. When I returned to my hotel room, my suits were not only there, but they had been unpacked and were hanging in my closet. A note on the bed indicated that I was a "distressed traveler" and that the airline would pay for my room. I went down to the restaurant, ate a good supper, and drank a brandy Alexander (the answer to a question in the practice game earlier that day, specifically, "You add one ounce of heavy cream and one ounce of crème de cacao to brandy to make this sweet cocktail"). I returned to the room and promptly fell asleep at eight o'clock. I awoke twelve hours later feeling on the top of the world. What a difference a day makes!

PART II

Playing Like a Champion

This section takes you to the podium to play the game itself. Learn how to master the buzzer, pick the categories, phrase your answer, bet on Daily Doubles, and come out of Final Jeopardy! the winner!

CHAPTER **5**

You're in Control

It is finally time. Five minutes before you need to go onstage and strut your intellectual stuff before the world, the contestant coordinators will call your name and the name of the other contestant who will face the champ. You get a few minutes for final preparations, and then you are led to the sound stage.

Stepping Up to the Podium

The first thing you do on the stage is go to the podium to sign your name. After you finish writing your name, you take your spot offstage, ready for your grand entrance. On the show at home, you see the contestants stroll to the podiums from offstage. It looks like a simple thing, and it probably would be if you were able to think clearly. But when the *Jeopardy!* music starts and Johnny Gilbert's voice comes on, your heart will be beating like crazy.

In addition, if you are shorter than average, like me, you will have to stand on a box. Apparently, the producers like the contestants to appear to be the same height, to avoid too much movement when the camera pans. In my fourth game, for example, I played against Joe, a polished gentleman who had been a carrier pilot in the navy. He was at least six-foot-two, so I had to stand on a six-inch-high box. I was worried they were going to have to stack two of them—and thankful they didn't.

***JEOPARDY!* SECRET NO. 11**
Jeopardy! likes the contestants to appear the same height on TV. Thus, the shorter ones have to stand on boxes.

When you get to the podium, after you have stared into the camera with the appropriate deer-caught-in-the-headlights smile, you should take a deep breath and quickly go over in your mind your goals for playing the game.

But what are they? This chapter will teach you some of the secrets of actually playing the game. You will learn about picking categories to throw off your competitors, how to use all your time when answering, and how to phrase your answers to avoid dumb errors. But first, we start with what is probably the single most important advice I can give you: how to win on the buzzer.

Mastering the Buzzer

If you carefully watch the hands of the players on any episode of *Jeopardy!*, you will see that on 90 percent of the questions, all three are ringing in, hoping their light will go on. It's the one who knows how to press that button at the right time who wins. I think I know the secret, so here's my take on the buzzer.

The Basics of the Buzzer

Let's start with the basics. The buzzer is a 4.5-inch-long cylinder with a cross-sectional diameter of 1.5 inches. (Yes, it feels very large in your hand.) It is connected to the computer inside each podium by a long, flexible wire. The wire is long enough to allow you to put your hand behind your back if you want. In the top center of the cylinder is a small white button with a surprising amount of springiness to it. To give an answer, you press that button, and I suggest that when you try to get in, you press it as much as possible.

On *Jeopardy!*, a player cannot ring in until Alex has finished reading the question. The way *Jeopardy!* accomplishes this is by stationing a production assistant offstage and arming him with a device with a button on it. When the assistant feels that Alex is through reading the question, he presses his button and two things happen simultaneously. Small pinlights in the middle of panels surrounding the playing board go on, and an electrical impulse is sent to the buzzers, activating them.

If you press your button before the assistant presses his, you really do get locked out for a fifth of a second. If you keep ringing in before the lockout is over, you keep getting locked out, I think, but the total lockout time does not seem to exceed about a second. (I am guessing from experience; I have not talked to any *Jeopardy!* techies about this.)

JEOPARDY! SECRET NO. 12

Players may not ring in until Alex has finished reading the question. If players come in too soon, they are locked out for 1/5 of a second.

The trick, therefore, is to ring in as soon after the assistant presses his button as possible, without coming in too early. Thus, even though Alex constantly calls players "fast" when they're good on the buzzer, the key is not speed but timing. And there are three keys to good *Jeopardy!* timing: accuracy, preparation, and adjustments.

Key No. 1: Accuracy

As any good baseball hitter will tell you, the key to timing is reducing extraneous movement in your swing, or in this case your buzz. Wade Boggs can be extremely accurate about when he swings at a pitch because his swing is so compact. With so

little extraneous body movement, he can fine-tune the timing of
his swing in a way that Cecil Fielder, a notorious free swinger,
can never do.

On *Jeopardy!*, you should strive to ring in by moving nothing
but your thumb, and you should move your thumb as little as
possible. I saw some people in my first five games who played
with their thumbs not touching the white button at the start of
the question. They probably were hoping this would help their
timing, the way some hitters use a hitch in their swing.

The problem was that they couldn't put their finger the same
distance and angle above the white button every time. Thus, they
introduced an element of error into their buzz. If they tried to
make a timing adjustment in one direction, their misplaced
thumb would actually change their timing in the other direction.

The same, I believe, is true of players who hold the buzzer up
instead of resting their hand on the podium or their hip. First,
they never hold their arm at the same angle every time,
changing their timing on every question. Second, with their arm
free-floating like that, they tend to do a windup with their
bodies before ringing in. The amount of windup they do is
going to change every time, and so will their timing.

I suggest standing close to the podium with your buzzer hand
resting on the podium in some comfortable way. This anchors
your hand and eliminates much body motion. There is a small
amount of space on the podium's surface in between the player
and the edge of the place where you write during Final
Jeopardy! Once you have put your hand there, take a deep
breath and consciously relax your body. You would be amazed at
the difference it makes.

When I was up there, I rested my hand on the podium in a
position I found comfortable. My thumb was on the white
button, putting slight pressure on it, but not enough to actually
move it. Then, when I perceived that Alex had finished reading,
I tried to ring in with only a downward thrust of my thumb, not
up and then down. I then pressed that button as much as
possible. (Perfect body posture and timing are only important to

the first press of the button each question. After you've started ringing in, do whatever is necessary with your body in order to press that button as frequently as possible for the next second or two.) The bottom line, though, is accuracy for that first press of the buzzer each question. You have to be able to press the button the same way every time.

Key No. 2: Preparation

I don't mean study like mad ahead of time (although that is imporant too). What I mean here is that you should train yourself to read all the way to the bottom of the question as soon as it flashes up on the screen. Don't just let Alex read the question to you while you read along.

By the time Alex has finished reading, you must have your answer ready in your mind and you must be focusing on the last word in the question. This was my biggest mistake during the Tournament of Champions. I would lose concentration and let Alex start reading to me, and I invariably got beat to the buzzer when I did that. So when you are at home watching the show, force yourself to read all the way to the bottom every time and have your answer in mind before Alex finishes reading. Then all you need to do is concentrate on the last word and Alex's voice. This is *very* important; at least it was to me.

TIP FROM THE CHAMP When you watch the show at home, get into the habit of reading all the way to the bottom of each question before Alex does. Don't just let him read it to you.

Note that I did not mention anything about waiting for the pinlights that surround the board to come on. The contestant coordinators will tell you all about those lights and about how you should wait for them to come on before ringing. If you do that you will not win. I have never heard of a Tournament of Champions competitor who relied on those lights (and I have talked to twenty of them). You must time it off Alex's voice alone.

Key No. 3: Adjustments

As I said before, the buzzers are activated by a human being, not some computer. Therefore, the timing will change throughout a day or even a game as that person tires or loses concentration. You have to be able to make adjustments. This was the key to my comeback in the second game of the finals at the Tournament of Champions. Also, if you are not getting in on the low-dollar questions at the start of a game, don't be afraid to make adjustments. I noticed that I needed to add a heartbeat of delay after I perceived Alex finishing the question in order to ring in first without being locked out. If you seem to be getting beat every time, then don't forget to try coming in *later* as one of your adjustments. Timing is highly individual. You need to find the right timing for you; everyone will perceive Alex finishing the question at a different time.

Many people, including Alex Trebek, have gone on and on about how fast I was on the buzzer. In reality, raw speed has nothing to do with it. It is not speed that wins on *Jeopardy!* but timing. You have to get into a rhythm—read to the bottom, get your answer in mind, focus on the last word, wait for Alex to finish, add whatever delay is necessary, then buzz, buzz, buzz like a madman (or woman). With luck, your little white lights will come on every time.

Ask for a Buzzer Check

Let me give you one last piece of advice about the buzzer. When you get to the podium, ask John Lauderdale, the stage manager, to do a buzzer check to see if your buzzer is working. For some reason, I asked for one right before the first final game of the Tournament of Champions—and the buzzer did not work! That was not the only time that the buzzers have not worked perfectly. Once or twice a season, you see a contestant on the show who had been on before. Sometimes Alex will refer to "technical difficulties" when explaining why the player is coming back. For example, you may have noticed that contestant

Claudia Perry appeared twice on the show in 1996. She experienced buzzer problems during her first show, and *Jeopardy!* had her back. Her story turned out fine—she went on to win four games—but it might not have. So I recommend that you request a buzzer check every time.

How to Answer Questions on *Jeopardy!*

Now that you are a master on the buzzer, you probably should make sure that you know how to answer once you are recognized. I'm not just talking about phrasing your response in the form of a question. Instead, I want to share with you two strategies that might get you two or three more correct answers per show. More important, they might be the only things that keep you from looking really foolish.

Take Your Time

Remember, you get about five seconds to answer once you ring in. I recommend that you use all of your time. Blurting out the answer as soon as you are recognized can result in a dumb error. For example, how many times have you seen a contestant answer a question in a category like *C* in Geography, in which all the answers are supposed to begin with *C,* and give an answer that does not begin with that letter? The person simply did not take a second to make sure her answer fit the category.

Thus, you *should* hesitate after Alex recognizes you and go over the answer in your head. First, does the answer you have fit the category? The answer in the category "Kings Named Haakon" will not be Henry VIII. Second, make sure that your answer is appropriate for the level of the question. For example, if the question is a $100 question about Shakespeare's plays, the answer is much more likely to be *Hamlet* rather than *Titus Andronicus.* Third, look for any words in quote marks in the question. In the following example, the word "colorful" is in quotes, which indicates that the answer has something to do with a color. The answer is Red Skelton.

Best known for playing
Freddie the Freeloader,
this "colorful"
comedian died in 1997

The quote marks indicate that the
answer has something to do with
a color.

It might seem unrealistic to think that you can actually go through all three mental steps in less than five seconds, but if you practice doing so at home, you will find that it becomes almost automatic. Again, this is why it is important to practice at home as if you are actually playing the game. It will become second nature to you, I promise.

THREE THINGS TO DOUBLECHECK BEFORE GIVING YOUR ANSWER

- Does your answer fit the category?
- Does your answer fit the dollar amount?
- Does your answer fit any punny clues in the question?

Every time you answer on the show, and while you are practicing at home, go through the mental checklist above. After a while, it will come second nature.

I also promise that if you think through your answer before giving a response, you will avoid many dumb errors. More than that, though, by controlling the flow of time you will feel generally more in control of the whole game. Also, I did not realize it at the time, but it drives your opponents nuts when you hesitate before you answer. They get their hopes up that you are going to miss, and then you whip out "What is the Gulf of Bothnia?" at the last second. Such ups and downs might be demoralizing to your opponents.

Give as Little Information as Possible

The second trick in answering questions is to give as little information as possible when answering the question. Giving the least amount of information presents the least opportunity for you to be wrong. This is an old College Bowl trick taught me by my venerable coach Lloyd Busch at Emory University. When a clue asks for a person, give only the last name. When it asks for a king, try not to give the number until Alex asks for it. Sometimes he won't.

When I was on the show, for example, I probably answered over one hundred questions that asked me for a person's name. In all of those cases but one, I gave only the last name. It saved my skin a few times, especially when in the finals of the Tournament of Champions the question asked for the British actor who played Ashley Wilkes in the movie *Gone With the Wind*. I knew the last name was Howard, but I could not remember whether it was Trevor or Leslie Howard. (I had managed to exclude Ken Howard of TV's *White Shadow* fame.) I had concluded that it was Trevor but remembered at the last minute to say only the last name. I responded, "Who is Howard?" and Alex said, "Right. Leslie Howard." My smile of relief is plainly visible on the tape.

Another time, though, I violated the last-names-only rule and it cost me. The clue concerned the inventor of the geodesic dome. I knew that it was a guy whose last two names were Buckminster Fuller, but I did not know whether "Buckminster" was a first name, a middle name, or part of a hyphenated last name. If I said his full name, I reasoned, I wouldn't have to worry about what "Buckminster" was. So I responded, "Who is Art Buckminster Fuller?" Alex accepted my answer, but during a commercial break the judges replayed the tape and noticed that I had said "Art." They informed Alex and me that his name is R. (for Richard) Buckminster Fuller, not "Art." The last name "Fuller" alone would have been sufficient, the judges also said. Thus, if I had followed the rule, I would have gotten it.

Picking the Next Category

After you have answered correctly, you will be called upon to choose the next category and dollar amount. Even here, there are several strategies you can employ to your advantage. I urge you to use them.

General Rule: Pick From Top to Bottom

The *Jeopardy!* folks want you to pick the questions in each category from the top to the bottom. This makes it easier to follow the questions with the camera and makes the board look better as they remove the used questions. And there are several reasons why picking from top to bottom can be beneficial to you.

First, sometimes you might get an oddly named category, and you might not be immediately able to figure out what it is all about. For example, the category "April Fools" came up during the first game when I was in the studio. The category ended up being about people born on April 1, but you could not tell this from the name. It's better to waste a $100 question to figure out the theme of the category than to miss out on a $500 one.

Second, some categories have a hidden theme. In one game I discussed earlier, the top four questions in the rightmost category had the following responses: "club, heart, diamonds, and spade." The $500 clue was "all the clues above relate to these objects." Imagine your confusion if you picked the $500 clue first.

The final reason to pick from top to bottom is that getting into a rhythm is one of the most important keys to your timing. Simply put, it's easier to keep your rhythm if you do not have to think about what category to pick next.

When to Break the Rule

There are, however, a couple of scenarios in which you should not simply pick top to bottom. First, if you are behind and there is not a great deal of time left, you might want to go for the big-money questions at the bottom of the board. This allows you to make up the difference faster. Also, the Daily Doubles appear most often in the bottom three rows of each board. Getting one of these can turn a game around quickly. That is why you sometimes see contestants in the Tournament of Champions start by picking from the bottom three rows. If you do want to try to find the Daily Doubles, though, I recommend that you do not do so until you have some money. Getting a Daily Double as the first pick of the game does not have much impact.

A second reason to avoid picking top to bottom is to employ what Chuck Forrest, winner of the second Tournament of Champions, called "the Rubin bounce" (after his law school classmate at the University of Michigan Law School, who suggested it). As I discussed with regard to the buzzer, it is essential to focus on the question as soon as it appears and then to read it beginning-to-end even before Alex reads it. If the person picking the category chooses totally at random, she knows exactly where to look but her opponents do not. They have to look to the top row, where the categories are listed, and then look down the column to find the right dollar value. Michael Daunt played this tactic against me in the finals of the Tournament of Champions, and I must admit that it was pretty effective.

You might also want to try to confuse your opponents with a trick Karl Coryat, the top single-game winner of 1996, used to great effect when picking categories. When a category is pretty specific—like "British Literature" or "Crossword Clues 'R'"—simply say "Literature" or "Crossword Clues" without being specific. You will know that it refers to British literature, but your opponents might forget. They either have to look at the top of the board, or they might even forget the category and give a nonfitting answer.

Pick Your Strong Categories First

There is one other consideration when picking categories. Using the buzzer is all about confidence and timing. You want to have the rhythm and the confidence, and you do not want your competitors to have them. Thus, if you get a chance to pick the category early in the game, I recommend that you start with your strong categories.

It will be easier this way to get into a rhythm from the beginning and may frustrate your opponents and make them begin to panic. Once you get to your weaker categories, you will be able to beat the others to any questions in those categories that you know. Even if your opponents get more than you here, they will simply be playing catch-up, so their confidence will not build up as much as it would otherwise. Thus, as soon as the categories are revealed, evaluate your strong and weak categories and plan out how and when you will go through them.

After reading this chapter, you should get in quite often in your games. Eventually, you will pick a Daily Double and hopefully you'll be in contention going into Final Jeopardy! The next chapter reveals the best betting strategies on Daily Doubles and in Final Jeopardy!

CHAPTER **6**

The Basics of Betting

Betting on Daily Doubles

Eventually, as you pick questions, you will get a Daily Double. While this is a great chance to turn the game your way, you also risk shooting yourself in the foot with a foolish bet. This section takes the randomness out of the betting process, as I show you simple principles that allow you to risk only the exact amount necessary to increase your odds of winning.

You've just correctly answered the $600 question in the category "The Caribbean." You realize the second Daily Double is still out there and you're $1,200 behind the leader. You pick the $800 question and hold your breath. Suddenly, the board explodes with sound and color and the crowd goes nuts. You got it! But now what do you do?

First, here's something you *don't* do. Don't let Alex rush you. Almost certainly, Alex will suggest—more or less seriously— that you bet it all. He will comment on your chances to take the lead or say that you have "a lot of money" and urge you to make a big wager. It's part of his job to keep the show moving, so he will also prompt you right away, and you may feel rushed. Don't let it throw you. This is your money, potentially, and you get as long as you want (within reason) to make your wager. Don't worry about how it will look at home; before the show airs, they will edit out any excess time.

When it comes to determining the amount to bet, your decision depends upon three things:

- How well you know the category
- How the buzzer is treating you
- How this wager can position you for Final Jeopardy!

When you think about a wager, the first consideration is, of course, your expertise in a certain category. I would never make a big wager in "Ballet," for example, but I'd bet the farm in "World Capitals," having memorized them all. You also want to remember that the difficulty of the questions on the *Jeopardy!* board increases with the dollar value, so a daily double under a $200 square is easier than one under a $500 question.

The next consideration is how the game is going for you, particularly on the buzzer. If you are being beaten to the buzzer almost every time, then the Daily Double might just be your only chance to win, so you should bet a great deal on it. On the other hand, if you are dominating on the buzzer, make a conservative bet. Why give your opponents a perfect chance to get back into the game?

If you feel pretty confident about a category and the buzzer is treating all three of you equally, you should view betting on Daily Doubles as a way to put yourself into the Final Jeopardy! scenario that gives you the most potential winning outcomes.

It's All About Final Jeopardy! Scenarios

Because positioning yourself for Final Jeopardy! should be your primary concern when betting on Daily Doubles, let's turn now to a discussion of how to bet in Final Jeopardy! Below are the six scenarios you might find yourself in going into the Final Jeopardy! round. Practice determining which scenario is presented in every game you watch at home. Try to guess what each player will bet.

THE SIX POSSIBLE FINAL JEOPARDY! SCENARIOS

Name of scenario	Scores going into Final Jeopardy!	Possible results	Proper bets
Lockout	2nd place player's score is less than 1/2 leader's score.	The leader should win every time.	*Leader:* Don't pull a Claven. Double the 2nd place score and subtract it from yours. Bet one dollar less than the difference. *Other players:* You're playing for 2nd place here.
Tie	2nd place player's score is exactly 1/2 leader's score.	The leader will come back for sure if she bets right, but will have company if the 2nd place player gets it right.	*Leader:* Bet zero. If two players tie for the lead and it's not a 0–0 tie, they both get the cash and come back as co-champions. *2nd place:* Bet it all.
Crush	2nd place score is between 1/2 and 2/3 of leader's score.	The leader will win unless she misses *and* 2nd place gets it.	*Leader:* Bet enough to beat the 2nd place player by a dollar if 2nd place doubled her money. *2nd place:* Bet it all. Since you have to answer correctly to win, you might as well play to win a lot.
Two-thirds	2nd place score is more than 2/3 of leader's score.	In 99% of the games where this scenario occurs, the leader bets enough to have one dollar more than the 2nd place player if the 2nd place player doubles her money. The leader will win if she gets it but should lose if she misses and 2nd place bets right.	*Leader:* Bet enough to beat the second player by a dollar if 2nd place player doubled her money. *2nd place:* Bet only so much that if you miss it you will still have more than the leader if she makes the usual bet and misses.

Prisoner's dilemma	Two players are tied for the lead going into Final Jeopardy! and the third player is not a factor	Who knows? Both people would be guaranteed to win if each bets zero. But do you trust the guy one podium over?	*Leaders:* Bet zero; Merv's got enough for everybody.
Tortoise and the hares	Two players are tied for the lead going into Final Jeopardy! and the third player has more than 1/2 their scores.	If two leaders stand pat and third guy gets it, he will have more than their scores, so leaders have to bet. Since both have to bet, they have to bet against each other.	*Leaders:* You basically have to bet it all to stay up with the other leader. *Third player:* Bet enough to have more than a leader who bets zero.

In your dream game, you enter Final Jeopardy! not only leading but with at least twice the score of the second-place competitor. This is the lockout scenario.

THE BEST FINAL JEOPARDY! SCENARIO:
YOU HAVE THE OTHERS LOCKED OUT

Scores going into Final Jeopardy!

You	*2ⁿᵈ place*	*3ʳᵈ place*
$10,000	$3,000	$1,000

If you have $10,000, second place has $3,000, and third place has $1,000, you are in great shape. In this scenario, even if the second-place player bets it all and gets the answer right, she will only have $6,000. Since you start with $10,000, even if you respond incorrectly, you are assured of victory—unless you beat yourself by betting too much.

Keep the lockout scenario in mind when betting on Daily Doubles. If you have more than twice the second-place score, multiply the second-place score by two. Then, do not bet so much on the Daily Double that you will have less than the resulting figure if you miss. Here's an example:

DON'T BET THE FARM ON A DAILY DOUBLE
WHEN YOU ALREADY HAVE THE OTHERS LOCKED OUT

Scores when you get a Daily Double late in the game

You	2nd Place	3rd Place
$10,000	$4,500	$500

In this example, if the game ended right there, the most the second player could have after Final Jeopardy! would be $9,000. You already have $10,000, so you should not bet any more than $999 on either a late-game Daily Double or Final Jeopardy!

This bet is pretty obvious, but some of the other Final Jeopardy! scenarios are less easy to recognize. For example, if you and the other players have the following scores at the end of the Double Jeopardy! round, what should you bet in Final Jeopardy!?

WHAT WOULD YOU BET IN THIS
FINAL JEOPARDY! SCENARIO?

Scores going into Final Jeopardy!

Leader	You	3rd Place
$9,000	$7,000	$1,500

Here, the leader has more than you do. Therefore, if the leader bets it all and gets it right you cannot win, even if you bet it all and get the question right as well.

So should you bet it all? No! As you will see, betting it all takes away a chance for you to win—for no reason. The key is that we know what the leader is probably going to do in this situation. We can place a cagey bet based on that knowledge.

How the Leader Bets 99 Percent of the Time

If you watch *Jeopardy!* and keep track, you will see that in 99 percent of the games the leader will bet enough to beat the second-place player's score by a dollar if the second-place player were to bet it all and respond correctly. In other words, the leader will multiply the second-place score by two and add a dollar, then bet enough to reach that figure with the right answer.

Let's check the leader's math for the scores above. If she bets $5,001 and gets it right, she will have $9,000 + $5,001 = $14,001. The most you can get is $14,000, so she has you locked out if you both answer correctly, even if you bet it all. So is there any reason to risk it all in this situation? No. However, once you realize that 99 percent of the people who are leading going into Final Jeopardy! will bet this way, you can place a smart bet from second place that greatly increases your chances of winning. Let's look at those scores again:

BETTING TO WIN FROM SECOND PLACE IN THIS FINAL JEOPARDY! SCENARIO

Scores going into Final Jeopardy!

Leader	You	3rd Place
$9,000	$7,000	$500

We are going to assume, as you should when you're up there, that the leader will bet enough to beat you by a dollar if you both get the answer right and you bet it all. Let's compare what will happen with different bets by you.

First, here are your chances of winning from second place if you bet it all:

CHANCES OF WINNING FROM SECOND PLACE IF YOU BET IT ALL AND YOU HAVE THE SCORES SHOWN ABOVE

What happens in Final Jeopardy!	Leader's score	2nd Place score	Result
Leader gets it, you miss it	$14,001	$0	You LOSE
Leader gets it, you get it	$14,001	$14,000	You LOSE

| Leader misses it, you miss it | $3,999 | $0 | You LOSE |
| Leader misses it, you get it | $3,999 | $14,000 | You WIN |

As you can see, if you bet it all and the leader bets the way we expect her to, you can only win in one Final Jeopardy! outcome—if the leader misses and you don't. But here are your chances of winning from second place if you bet zero:

ODDS OF WINNING FROM SECOND PLACE IF YOU BET NOTHING AND YOU HAVE THE SCORES SHOWN ABOVE

What happens in Final Jeopardy!	Leader's score	2nd Place score	Result
Leader gets it, you miss it	$14,001	$7,000	You LOSE
Leader gets it, you get it	$14,001	$7,000	You LOSE
Leader misses it, you miss it	$3,999	$7,000	You WIN
Leader misses it, you get it	$3,999	$7,000	You WIN

If you look at the last column of the charts, you see that when your second-place score is high enough, you have two chances of winning in Final Jeopardy! if you bet nothing but only one chance of winning if you bet the whole thing. Thus, in certain scenarios, second place should bet nothing or very little.

However, in other situations, your second-place score is not enough to make this strategy work for you. Consider what happens in the following scenario:

CAN YOU BET ZERO FROM SECOND PLACE IN THIS FINAL JEOPARDY! SCENARIO?

Scores going into Final Jeopardy!

Leader	You	3rd Place
$9,000	$5,000	$1,000

First, let's determine what the leader will bet in 99 percent of the cases. She will bet enough to end up with $10,001, which is your score doubled plus one dollar. Starting with $9,000, she needs to bet $1,001. With that bet, if she misses, she will still have $7,999, which is more than you started with. Thus, you are not in the zero-bet scenario, since you must get the Final Jeopardy! question right to win.

Two-thirds Is the Magic Number

You might be wondering, at this point, how high your score must be compared to the leader's to put you into the zero-bet scenario. If you plug the leader's score (P_1) and the second-place score (P_2) into an algebraic formula to figure this out, the wonderfully complex equation looks something like this:

$$\text{You should bet zero if: } P_2 > P_1 - \{[\,(P_2 * 2) + 1] - P_1\}$$

Who could ever remember this formula in thirty seconds?

Ouch! Imagine trying to remember that formula in thirty seconds. Lucky for you, I've reduced the equation and determined that it comes down to this simple rule of thumb:

$$\text{You should bet zero if: } P_2 > 2/3 \text{ of } P_1$$

Luckily, the formula reduces to this simple rule of thumb.

This is the "two-thirds" rule. That is, if you go into Final Jeopardy! in second place, you should bet zero if your score is greater than two-thirds of the leader's score. For an example, let's take a case right at the border.

If the leader has $9,000 and you have $6,000, then you are just within the two-thirds scenario. The leader will probably bet enough to have $12,001, which means she has to risk $3,001. If she misses, she will have only $5,999, and this is less than you start with ($6,000). So you should bet nothing in Final Jeopardy!

The Two-thirds Rule Can Win Games

I am not just being theoretical here; this rule can win games for you. The best example of this in my experience occurred during my semifinal game in the Tournament of Champions. I faced two very tough opponents. One was Shane Whitlock, the college champion and a microbiology major from Arkansas who was blazingly fast on the buzzer. The other was the implacable Dr. Bev Spurs, a podiatrist from England who seemed to know everything and had nerves of steel.

When the game began, I realized that I was going to have big problems winning it. During my five regular games and my quarterfinal, I could always rely on sheer speed to get me out of jams. Also, during the five regular-season games at least, I had more depth of knowledge than my opponents. In this game, though, Shane had all the speed and Bev had all the depth. To make it worse, "Actors," "Business," and "Proverbs" came up, and they are not good categories for me.

In the first half, I struggled just to stay afloat. I simply could not get in on the ones I knew, and I made bad guesses on those I could get in on. For the product that contains "retsin," for example, I guessed "What is Pam?" instead of "What is Certs?" I was not playing my best, that's for sure.

Bev was in charge and I was in third going into Double Jeopardy! That meant I picked first—"Poetry," one of my strong categories. As I suggested in the previous chapter, I picked my strong categories at the beginning of the round, trying to build up momentum. I got four out of five, and I was closing the gap.

But all of a sudden, Shane came alive and went on a killer streak. He must have gotten eight out of ten in a row, including both Daily Doubles. By the time I looked up, he had over $10,000. Meanwhile, I was having severe concentration problems. I found myself looking at my little white indicator lights, hoping they would come on, instead of looking at the board. I was beginning to panic, wondering if Shane was going to coast right into the lockout scenario.

Then, a question came up asking which Mexican-American War hero led the Union troops right before the Civil War began. I had just studied the Civil War and kind of thought I remembered it being Winfield Scott. The score was getting out of hand, so I rang in and guessed. I was right.

I was so tickled at remembering him that I smiled, took a deep breath, and finally relaxed. As soon as I did that, my timing on the buzzer came back. I started picking questions from the bottom of the board and guessing at every turn. I must have guessed three $1,000 answers in a row.

I felt that I had nothing to lose. By this point, I was pretty sure I would not have *less* than half Shane's score or have *more* than Shane's total score. What I wanted to ensure was that I had at least two-thirds of Shane's score so that I would be in the two-thirds scenario.

As it turned out, my comeback drive brought me well beyond the two-thirds point. In fact, when I looked at the final scores, my first pained thought was that if I hadn't stupidly guessed "What is Pam?" in the first half, I would have been leading going into Final Jeopardy! As it was, I fell just a tiny bit short. Shane had $11,500, I had $11,100, and Bev had $5,500. I was in the two-thirds scenario.

The best thing to do in the two-thirds scenario is to bet enough to cover the leader's zero bet, if you can afford to. But because Bev had $5,500, I had to bet less than $100. You see, even if she doubled her score, to $11,000, she would still have $100 less than what I started with. With a less-than-$100 bet, I wouldn't have to risk her catching me from below.

So I knew immediately that I needed to bet less than $100; I couldn't even cover a zero bet by Shane. However, I made sure to ask—in an easily heard voice—for scratch paper, to ostensibly figure out my bet. (I wanted to make Shane think I was betting something, to preclude a zero bet from him, like the one Rachel Schwartz used to beat Kurt Bray in the semis in 1994.)

So I placed my zero bet and prayed that the question would be hard, hard, hard. When the clue came up, I was moderately hopeful. The question was about the river that explorers once thought originated in "the Mountains of the Moon."

I knew the answer immediately, "The Nile," but then, "Geography" was my absolute best category. Maybe they wouldn't know, I hoped. Then, I remembered that there had been some movie about this. No, I thought, they'll know it for sure.

Incidentally, although I knew the answer to this one, when I made my bet I decided to write my daughter's name instead of the answer, because no one gives you grief for betting nothing if you then miss. (I bet nothing once before, you may remember.) After I saw the clue, I had to resist the overwhelming impulse to put the right answer down. It felt like sacrilege to miss a Jeopardy! question on purpose. But I superstitiously felt that if I wrote it—or even thought about it too much—the thought would somehow make its way over to Shane.

When they revealed Bev's answer, hope leapt in my heart. She had put "What is the Ganges?" "Ganges" was a great guess—the one I think I would have made if I had not known the specific fact. I mean, the Himalayas are so high one could very fittingly call them the Mountains of the Moon. Boy, that was logical, I thought, but would Shane think so too? As they moved to Shane, he had a great poker face, although he already knew he had lost. I couldn't read anything in his expression, so I decided to look straight ahead, eyes closed, and just listen for Alex to read his answer.

I never imagined I'd be so thrilled to hear someone say "Ganges." It was the only time I have ever had tears in my eyes from sheer happiness and relief. Shane had bet $11,000 of his $11,500 (in order to have more than I would even if I got the answer right and doubled my $11,100.) Thus, he had only $500 left after he missed, while I still had my whole $11,100. Thus, through a little good strategizing, I won this semifinal match from second place.

Back to Betting on Daily Doubles

I put this discussion of Final Jeopardy! betting right in the middle of talking about Daily Doubles for a reason. When you

are betting on Daily Doubles, especially late in the game, you
should always keep in mind the Final Jeopardy! scenario you are
in at that moment and try to get into a better one without risking
getting into a worse.

For example, let's imagine you get a Daily Double late in the
game when you have $5,500 and the leader has $9,000. You fall
into the scenario of having between half and two-thirds of the
leader's score. You would like to take the lead, and you could if
you bet $3,501. But if you missed you would only have $1,999,
making you the loser in the lockout scenario.

A better bet here would be $500. If you get the answer right, you
have $6,000, exactly what you need to put you in the more desir-
able two-thirds scenario. If you get it wrong, you will have $5,000,
which is still between half and two-thirds of the leader's score.
Thus, you might increase your odds of winning in Final Jeopardy!
and you don't have to risk decreasing your chances of winning.

Bet to Improve Your Scenario

A frequent error that drives me nuts is made when a second-
place player in the two-thirds scenario bets (a) enough to take
himself out of the two-thirds scenario if he misses but (b) not
enough to take the lead if he responds correctly. For example, a
second-place player actually made the following bet on a Daily
Double that was revealed on the last question of a game with
these scores:

WHAT WOULD YOU BET ON THIS DAILY DOUBLE?

Scores when you get the Daily Double on the last
question of the game

Leader	You	3ʳᵈ Place
$9,000	$7,100	$1,000

There were no questions left besides the Daily Double, so she
knew that her bet determined how the players would line up in

Final Jeopardy! She bet $1,500. Now, looking back at the chart on page 75, let's see what her bet did for her.

At the moment she bet, she trailed but had over two-thirds of the leader's score. She was in the two-thirds scenario right then. After that bet, if she gets the Daily Double right, she will have $7,100 + $1,500 = $8,600. What scenario will she fall into then? The same one as when she started—she will trail the leader but have two-thirds or more of the leader's score. In other words, even if she gets the question right, she has not increased the number of Final Jeopardy! outcomes that result in her winning.

But if she misses the Daily Double question, what happens? She will have $7,100 − $1,500 = $5,600. That score takes her out of the two-thirds scenario and puts her into the scenario in which she has between half and two-thirds of the leader's score, allowing her to win only if she gets it and the leader misses. All that has to happen for the second-place person to win in the two-thirds scenario is for the leader to miss. In other words, by betting the way she did, the woman took the risk of eliminating one possibility of winning without increasing the possibility of winning if she got the Daily Double right.

She should have bet either to take the lead, by betting at least $1,901, or to remain in the two-thirds scenario if she missed. That is, she could have bet less than $1,100. Personally, I would have bet $2,900. If I got it, I would have $7,100 + $2,900 = $10,000 and the lead going into Final Jeopardy! The former leader would then be in the two-thirds scenario with respect to my score, and all I would need to do to win is to get Final Jeopardy! right.

But if I missed the Daily Double, I would then have $7,100 − $2,900 = $4,500. This is exactly half the leader's score going into Final Jeopardy! and would put us in the tie scenario. The leader would bet zero, and all I would have to do to come back as a co-champion is get the Final Jeopardy! question right. It would not matter whether the leader got the Final Jeopardy! question right.

Betting in the Two-thirds Scenario As the Leader

Let me give you one last way to snatch victory from the jaws of defeat. When you are the leader in the two-thirds scenario, don't bet enough to beat the second-place player by a dollar if her score is doubled. Instead, bet enough to tie her doubled score. Here's what I mean.

Assume that these are the scores going into Final Jeopardy!

SCORES GOING INTO FINAL JEOPARDY!

Leader	2nd Place	3rd Place
$9,000	$7,000	$500

If your opponent is familiar with the two-thirds scenario, she may figure out what you will bet and what you will have if you miss, and bet accordingly. She thinks you will bet $5,001, which is enough to have $14,001 if you get it right. That is one dollar more than the second-place player would have if she got it right and bet it all. If you were to bet this amount and get it wrong, you would be left with $9,000 − $ 5,001 = $ 3,999.

The second-place player might take that result, add one to it, and subtract it from her score: $3,999 + $1 = $4,000, and $7,000 − $4,000 = $3,000. That would be the amount she could bet and still win if you miss. If she were to bet $3,000 and you were to bet enough to beat her doubled score by a dollar, and you both missed, she would have $4,000 and you would have $3,999. She would win by a dollar.

But if you bet only enough to tie her doubled score, you would bet only $5,000. If you missed you would have $4,000 instead of $3,999. Thus, if you bet for the tie instead of the win, and then you both miss, both of you would have $4,000. You would return as co-champions, and you would both get the money.

As you can see, betting in Final Jeopardy! can be quite complex. Take heart, however. If you practice using the chart and the techniques offered in this chapter, before long betting will become second nature to you.

The important message of this chapter is that betting is not merely a mathematical guessing game. Instead, the idea behind betting on Daily Doubles is determining what Final Jeopardy! scenario you will be in if you get the answer right and if you get it wrong. The best wager on a Daily Double is one that will move you to a better scenario if you get it right but will not drop you to a worse scenario if you get it wrong.

In Final Jeopardy!, please do not forget the rule of two-thirds. Determine which scenario you are in and bet according to the directions given in the chart on pages 73–74. But most important, do not simply come up with a figure from thin air. Make sure that your bet helps you actually increase your chances of winning.

PART III

Learning the Facts

This section supplies all of the most important or hardest-to-find information that Jeopardy! likes to ask. Become an instant expert in fine art, literature, opera, cooking, and many other fields! Although these are questions I wrote, similar questions are bound to show up on the show itself.

Fine Arts

The categories covered in this chapter are included because they so often trip up potential champions. The facts below were selected because they are the ones that are most likely to come up.

SOURCES OF QUICK INFORMATION

The Dictionary of Cultural Literacy, pp. 155–89 (fine arts)

Marvin S. Shaw and Warren, Richard, A Viewer's Guide to Art: A Glossary of Gods, People and Creatures. (John Muir Publications, 1991)

The New York Public Library Desk Reference, 2d ed., chapter 7, "The Arts," pp. 127–201

An Incomplete Education, pp. 62–117 (art history), 262–99 (music)

Dance

What do you know about ballet and other kinds of dance? If you are like most people, very little. But *Jeopardy!* really only asks about the basics. Below you will find a list of the most famous figures in the history of dance. If you know these, you will go far if the subject comes up.

Top Ten Dance Figures Most Likely to Come Up on *Jeopardy!*

Vaslav Nijinsky	Star dancer of the Ballets Russes. His most noted performance was in *Rite of Spring,* which caused a riot at its premiere. Went insane and died in an asylum.
Sergei Diaghilev	A nondancer. Impresario who founded the Ballets Russes.
Rudolf Nureyev	A star of the Kirov Ballet until his 1961 defection to the West, after which he frequently paired with Margot Fonteyn. Known for his amazing leaps.
Jerome Robbins	Dancer and choreographer who often combined jazz, modern, and social dance. Choreographed and directed *West Side Story* and *Fiddler on the Roof* for Broadway. Long association with New York City Ballet; founder of Ballets: U.S.A.
Mikhail Baryshnikov	Member of Kirov Ballet until 1974, when he defected and joined the American Ballet Theater (artistic director from 1980 to 1989).
Isadora Duncan	One of the first figures of modern dance, she rejected rigid ballet in favor of expressive classically inspired dance. She died when a long scarf she was wearing got caught in a moving car's tire.
Martha Graham	In a career spanning a century, she created a rigorous technique including the "contraction." *Appalachian Spring* is her most well known work.
Agnes de Mille	Created works rooted in American folklore, including *Rodeo* and the dances for the Broadway musical *Oklahoma!*

Alvin Ailey	African-American choreographer. Combined African, modern, and jazz elements in his works, performed by his American Dance Theater.
George Balanchine	He worked with the Ballets Russes before cofounding New York City Ballet with Lincoln Kirstein in 1948. Favored plotless ballets with neoclassical themes such as *Agon* and *Apollo*.

Dance Terms

Plié	A bending of the knees in ballet
Jeté	A jump in which one leg is thrown to the side
Arabesque	Extension of one leg straight back 90 degrees with shoulders squared
Pirouette	A turn on one leg, with the toe of the other leg on the knee
Pas de deux	A dance for two, usually man and woman
Cabriole	A leap in which the lower leg beats against the upper one at an angle, before the dancer lands on the lower leg
Five positions	The basic positions of the feet in ballet

Quiz: The History and Art of Ballet

Q. Often partnered with Karsavina, he created the title role in Fokine's *Petrouchka* and choreographed himself in *Afternoon of a Faun*. A. Vaslav Nijinsky

Q. This American directed as well as choreographed *Bells Are Ringing* (1956), *West Side Story* (1957), *Gypsy* (1959), and *Fiddler on the Roof* (1964). A. Jerome Robbins

Q. This American tap dancer gained renown with his appearance in the revue *Blackbirds* in 1928 and later appeared in *The Little Colonel* with Shirley Temple. A. Bill "Bojangles" Robinson

Q. After a career with the Ballet Russe de Monte Carlo, and the New York City Ballet, she founded the Chicago City Ballet. A. Maria Tallchief

Q. After a distinguished dancing career with the Kirov Ballet and the Royal Ballet of England, he was the director of the Paris Opéra Ballet from 1983 to 1989. A. Rudolf Nureyev

Q. This ballet pioneer toured with the Ballets Russes before forming her own company, which introduced ballet to millions worldwide. A. Anna Pavlova

Q. This ballerina, known for her graceful and pliant arms, recently gave a tribute performance at the Bolshoi Ballet. A. Maya Plisetskaya

Q. His works such as *Revelations* and *Cry* blended African, jazz, and modern dance techniques and were performed at his American Dance Theater. A. Alvin Ailey

Q. This choreographer began with Martha Graham's troupe but left to produce avant-garde works such as *Events* and *Summerspace,* often with John Cage. A. Merce Cunningham

Q. Russian ballet was at its height when this Frenchman became ballet master at the Imperial Theater in St. Petersburg in 1862. A. Marius Petipa

Q. Before his defection in 1974, Baryshnikov was associated with this Russian ballet company. A. Kirov

Q. In 1909, this nondancer formed the Ballets Russes. A. Sergei Diaghilev

International Dance Quiz

Jeopardy! often asks about dances from around the world. See if you can identify the following international dances:

1. Social dance developed in Argentina in 4/4 time.
2. Dance in 3/4 time that developed from the *Landler,* a German-Austrian turning dance.
3. Nineteenth-century square dance in five sections, each with a different time.
4. Yes, Virginia, the Highland fling is a variation of this lively British dance for couples.
5. A Polish national dance in triple time with proud bearing, clicking of heels, and a special turning step.
6. A lively Spanish dance performed with castanets or tambourines.
7. A Sevillian gypsy dance accompanied by clapping or a guitar and characterized by its heelwork, or *taconeo.*
8. Raucous and outlawed dance performed in French music halls.
9. Turn-of-the-century African-American dance in which couples compete for a "sweet" prize.
10. General term for social dances done by couples, like the fox-trot, waltz, rumba, and cha-cha.

Answers on page 108.

Q. *Apollo, Agon, Serenade,* and *Jewels* are all neoclassical masterpieces by this choreographer.   A. George Balanchine

Q. Diaghilev commissioned this top choreographer with the Ballets Russes to create *The Firebird* and *Petrouchka.*
   A. Michel Fokine

Q. He started a riot when he choreographed and danced in the Paris premiere of *Rite of Spring*. A. Vaslav Nijinsky

Q. She was a Russian dancer with the Kirov before she defected and joined the American Ballet Theater; she later won a Tony for *On Your Toes*. A. Natalia Makarova

Q. After she joined the New York City Ballet in 1961, she became the "muse" of George Balanchine; he was devastated when she married a dancer in 1969. A. Suzanne Farrell

Q. Suzanne Farrell once danced the role of Dulcinea, opposite Balanchine himself as this title character. A. *Don Quixote*

Q. This current leader of the New York City Ballet began his career with the Royal Danish Ballet. A. Peter Martins

Q. After dancing with the New York City Ballet since the mid-1950s, Arthur Mitchell founded this black classical dance company in 1968. A. Dance Theater of Harlem

Q. From 1965 on, her work has included creating idiosyncratic modern pieces like *Deuce Coupe*, choreographing the movie *Hair*, and directing Broadway's *Singing in the Rain*. A. Twyla Tharp

Q. Her long dance career spanned the twentieth century and gave us *Appalachian Spring* and a rigorous dance technique centered on what she called "contraction." A. Martha Graham

Q. Her ballets rooted in American folklore include *Rodeo* and *Fall River Legend*; her Broadway choreographing included *Oklahoma!* A. Agnes de Mille

Q. One of the first figures in modern dance, this American rejected rigid ballet and looked to ancient Greece for inspiration for her expressive form of dance. A. Isadora Duncan

Q. Britain's first prima ballerina was this North London native, dubbed "the Child Pavlova." A. Alicia Markova

Q. In 1974, he joined the American Ballet Theater, which he later led for several years before leaving to form the White Oak Dance Project. A. Mikhail Baryshnikov

Q. He choreographed 1944's *Fancy Free* to Leonard Bernstein's music and worked with that composer again on 1957's *West Side Story*. A. Jerome Robbins

Q. Born Lillian Alicia Marks in North London, she Russianized her name to seem more exotic. A. Alicia Markova

Q. This choreographer worked with the Ballets Russes before forming the American School of Ballet in 1934. A. George Balanchine

Q. In 1948 Balanchine and Lincoln Kirstein started this ballet company, which is still going, under the directorship of Peter Martins. A. New York City Ballet

Q. She charged Anton Dolin, her former partner, and Diaghilev, her mentor at the Ballets Russes, with intentionally depriving her of a normal life. A. Alicia Markova

Q. The elegance and style of this married couple contributed to the spread of ballroom dancing before World War I. A. Vernon and Irene Castle

Q. After overcoming debt and inner strife, this ballet company settled into its new home in Chicago in 1996. A. Joffrey Ballet

Q. The father of this prima ballerina negotiated a treaty with the U.S. government creating the Osage reservation in Oklahoma; when oil was discovered, he became rich. A. Maria Tallchief

Q. In 1915, this pair founded the first modern dance school, whose name was a combination of their names. A. Ruth St. Denis and Ted Shawn (Denishawn was the school)

Q. This British ballet pioneer choreographed *Ondine* for Sadler's Wells Ballet, now the Royal Ballet of Britain. A. Sir Frederick Ashton

Q. Englishman Sydney Healey-Kay was better known by this name when partnering Alicia Markova. A. Anton Dolin

Q. Gerald Arpino became the artistic director of this ballet company in 1988. A. Joffrey

Q. Balanchine's 1949 production of *The Firebird* made this woman, his wife at the time, a star.   A. Maria Tallchief

Q. This British choreographer was associated with the American Ballet Theater and created intensely psychological ballets such as *Pillar of Fire*.   A. Antony Tudor

Q. He was a star of the Kirov Ballet until his 1961 defection to the West, after which he frequently paired with Margot Fonteyn.   A. Rudolf Nureyev

A Night at the Opera

If you ask people what their *Jeopardy!* nightmare is, a good number of them would reply, "Getting 'Opera' as the category for Final Jeopardy!" Yet many would be surprised how quickly they can bring themselves up to speed in this subject. Here are some questions with information that you should know about Music and Opera.

THE MOST IMPORTANT OPERA QUESTIONS

Q. This opera singer of Greek descent attempted to revive bel canto style in the 1950s.   A. Maria Callas

Q. Rossini's *Barber of Seville* is an example of this style of comic opera.   A. Opera buffa (or opéra bouffe)

Q. This Russian based operas on both *War and Peace* and *Romeo and Juliet*.   A. Sergei Prokofiev

Q. Seventeenth-century English composer of *Dido and Aeneas*.   A. Henry Purcell

Q. This New Zealand–born soprano is probably the only diva from that country.   A. Kiri Te Kanawa

Q. This early Italian opera composer created *Orfeo*, often considered the first opera.   A. Claudio Monteverdi

Q. This word refers to elaborate ornamentation in vocal music, or to a soprano who specializes in it.   A. Coloratura

Q. This Italian term was given to the "gutter realism" of Puccini's operas.   A. Verismo

Q. This German opera reformer drew on classical Greece for his best-known works. A. Christoph Willibald von Gluck

Q. This Mozart sexual farce scandalized audiences until late in the twentieth century. A. *Così Fan Tutte*

Q. His opera *Salome* was a succès de scandale; his *Der Rosenkavalier* was more conventional. A. Richard Strauss

Music and Opera Lingo

Jeopardy! likes to ask about the terms associated with classical music and opera. Here are some of the usual suspects.

Literally meaning "beautiful singing," it is a singer-dominated style of opera espoused by Maria Callas	Bel canto
Literally meaning a "goddess," it is the highest accolade given a singer, better even than "prima donna"	Diva
These speechlike passages advance the plot of an opera	Recitatives
This is the "little book" that accompanies an opera	Libretto
This term from the French refers to any opera with spoken dialogue, not just humorous ones	Opéra comique
Music with voice only, meaning "as in church"	A capella
An extended vocal solo, often a showcase for virtuosity	Aria
The male voice between bass and tenor	Baritone
Introduction to a large piece, such as an opera	Overture
A musical setting of scriptural text without costumes or action	Oratorio

Q. One-word title of an unfinished opera by Alban Berg.
A. *Lulu*

Q. This German went to Paris in the early 1800s, became the master of French opera, and composed the grand opera *Les Huguenots.* A. Giacomo Meyerbeer

Q. Brilliant, anti-Wagnerian French opera composer whose giant masterpiece was *Les Troyens* (*The Trojans*). A. Hector Berlioz

Q. Hector Berlioz's opera about this Florentine goldsmith was a resounding flop. A. Benvenuto Cellini

Q. His *Faust* is one of the few French operas performed around the world. A. Charles Gounod

Q. This British composer's operas based on literary works include *Death in Venice, Billy Budd,* and *The Turn of the Screw.* A. Benjamin Britten

Q. His only complete opera, *Boris Godunov,* is based on a play by Pushkin. A. Modest Moussorgsky

Q. This composer's *Eugene Onegin* has been criticized as being "too pretty." A. Peter Ilyich Tchaikovsky

Q. Most of this Czech's operas tended toward the heroic and nationalistic, but his most famous one is a peasant comedy, *The Bartered Bride.* A. Bedřich Smetana

Q. This Czech composer's love of nature and his obsession with folk idioms and speech rhythms are evident in *Jenoufa, The Makropoulos Affair,* and *Cunning Little Vixen.*
A. Leoš Janáček

Q. The composer of *Four Saints in Three Acts* and *The Mother of Us All* is this American. A. Virgil Thomson

Q. This opera is Menotti's melodramatic, supernatural thriller. A. *The Medium*

Q. This Christmas opera by Menotti was the first written specifically for television. A. *Amahl and the Night Visitors*

Q. Menotti's serious opera about religious skepticism concerned the "saint" of this street. A. Bleecker Street

Richard Wagner

A disproportionate amount of questions in Opera are about only four composers. Richard Wagner is one. Here's what you need to know about him.

English translation of term Wagner used to describe his works	Music dramas
A yearly Wagner festival is held in this German city	Bayreuth
Wagner's massive cycle of operas	*The Ring of the Niebelungs*
A recurring theme in a work, particularly Wagner's	Leitmotif
Wagnerian opera featuring a noted swan ride	*Lohengrin*
Wagner's father-in-law was this composer	Franz Liszt
This opera was Wagner's only comedy	*Die Meistersinger von Nürnberg*

Q. He collaborated with Robert Wilson to create *Einstein on the Beach,* a marathon work attempting to explain the theory of relativity in music. A. Phillip Glass

Q. The "Habanera" and "Toreador Song" are well-known excerpts from what opera about a woman who works in a cigarette factory and manipulates men? A. *Carmen*

Q. In what Verdi opera does Violetta, a courtesan, sing "Sempre libera"? A. *La Traviata*

Q. Phillip Glass's piece about Gandhi and passive resistance. A. *Satyagraha*

Q. In the Puccini opera *Tosca,* this was Tosca's profession. A. Singer

Q. What Puccini opera contains the aria "Vissi d'arte"?
A. *Tosca*

Q. What Verdi opera includes the aria "La donna è mobile"? A. *Rigoletto*

Q. What opera includes a famous "mad scene" at a wedding during which the bride stabs someone? A. *Lucia di Lammermoor*

Q. In what opera does a servant, Leporello, entertain a vengeful jilted lover by cataloguing his master's amorous conquests? A. *Don Giovanni*

Q. What opera involves a Druid woman's love for a Roman proconsul? A. *Norma*

Q. What character sings the famous "Flower Song" from *Carmen*? A. Don José

Q. English opera company that isn't the Royal Opera but still comes up on *Jeopardy!* A. Sadler's Wells (renamed the English National Opera in 1974)

Q. Literally "State Opera," this Viennese opera house is virtually the music capital of the world. A. Staatsoper

Q. The Festspielhaus is the opera house associated with this opera festival. A. Bayreuth

---

Giaccomo Puccini

Puccini is another *Jeopardy!* favorite. Surprisingly, this is the small group of facts they ask about.

Puccini opera about starving artists	La Bohème
Puccini opera about Japanese woman who falls for Western naval officer	Madame Butterfly
This name of the naval officer in *Madame Butterfly* is also that of a detective agency	Pinkerton
Puccini opera about singer harassed by evil police chief	Tosca
Unfinished last opera of Puccini, set in China	Turandot

Q. Name of the great Paris opera house. A. L'Opéra

Q. Opened in 1883, it was the brainchild of a group of businessmen who were irritated by not being able to get boxes at the Academy of Music in New York City. A. Metropolitan Opera

Q. His murals at the Metropolitan Opera draw both gasps and snickers. A. Marc Chagall

Q. The Metropolitan Opera is located in this complex. A. Lincoln Center for the Performing Arts

---

Giuseppe Verdi

After Puccini, Verdi is the operatic composer most often asked about. Master these facts and you'll get 90 percent of questions about Verdi.

Verdi opera whose title means literally "The Lost One"	La Traviata
Verdi opera whose title means literally "The Troubador"	Il Trovatore
Verdi's only comedy is based on this Shakespearean character (his other Shakespearean titles include Hamlet and Othello)	Falstaff
Verdi opera about a hunchback jester, which includes aria "La donna è mobile"	Rigoletto
Verdi opera about Violetta, a courtesan, and based on Dumas's La Dame aux Camélias	La Traviata
Verdi opera about an Egyptian princess, which was commissioned for the opening of the Suez Canal	Aida

---

The Classics and Classical Music

Classical music is a common *Jeopardy!* topic, and questions about it usually test one of two things. This first type of question asks you about things that someone who plays an instrument should know. The second type tests whether you know Prokofiev from Shostakovich; in other words, do you listen to classical music and know its major figures and their works? Contemporary music has also made its way into *Jeopardy!*'s classical music category. These questions cover scores from Broadway's Great White Way to Americana's stand-by classics. Here are some questions of each variety.

QUESTIONS FROM THE WORLD OF MUSIC

Q. Of grave, largo, and presto, which is the slowest speed of playing a piece of music?   A. Grave

Q. What Italian tenor of the early twentieth century was the first person to have a million-selling record?   A. Enrico Caruso

Q. What Polish-French composer was perhaps the greatest chamber pianist of all time?   A. Frederick Chopin

Q. Besides a piccolo, what is another high-pitched flute used primarily in military bands?   A. Fife

Q. From the Italian for "cheerful," what tempo notation indicates a piece should be played at a lively, brisk speed?   A. Allegro

Q. From the Italian for "tail," it comes at the end of a piece of music, or the title of a Led Zeppelin album. What is the four-letter word?   A. Coda

Q. From the Italian for "from the head," it means to repeat from the beginning. What is it?   A. Da capo

Q. What Italian version of the French word for "sliding" describes a one-finger sweep across a series of keys on the piano?   A. Glissando

Q. From the Italian for "bound together," it's the opposite of staccato.   A. Legato

Q. This musical term comes from the Italian for "pinched," and that is just what you do to the violin's strings when playing this way.   A. Pizzicato

Q. What American patriotic song begins, "O beautiful for spacious skies"? A. "America the Beautiful"

Q. What German organist and composer created the *Goldberg Variations?* A. Johann Sebastian Bach

Q. From the Italian for "detached," what musical term means to play the notes in an unconnected manner? A. Staccato

Q. This double-reed instrument is the second largest member of the woodwind family. A. Bassoon

Q. What playwright and lyricist teamed up with Richard Rodgers to make *Oklahoma!* and with Jerome Kern to make *Show Boat?* A. Oscar Hammerstein

Q. This Austrian composer and onetime teacher of Mozart was called "Papa" and wrote 104 classical symphonies. A. Franz Joseph Haydn

Q. In John Cage's *Imaginary Landscape No. 4,* twelve of what objects are played by twenty-four performers? A. Radios

Q. What instrument, which has the second lowest voice among the strings, is played by Yo-Yo Ma? A. Cello

Q. What composer created his famous *Chorale* Symphony while almost completely deaf? A. Ludwig van Beethoven

Q. He is probably the only German-born, naturalized English composer whose name will come up on *Jeopardy!* A. George Frideric Handel

Q. What American composer's *Rhapsody in Blue* was first performed by the Paul Whiteman orchestra? A. George Gershwin

Q. Of double, half, triple, or one-quarter: Which does "mezzo" mean when you see it in a musical score? A. Half

Q. The opposite of the adjective "piano," "forte" means to play a piece of music in what manner? A. Loudly

Q. This Italian term, often associated with Bach, describes a piece that shows off the player's "touch." A. Toccata

Q. From the Italian for "harp," this word means to play all the notes in a chord from top to bottom—or vice versa—one at a time? A. Arpeggio

Q. This Italian word for "wide" or "broad" indicates the second slowest tempo. A. Largo

Q. What composer created *The Messiah,* the oratorio that includes the famous "Hallelujah" chorus? A. George Frideric Handel

Q. This word, the Italian for "joke," is often applied to the third movement of a symphony. A. Scherzo

Q. What American songwriter gave us the memorable "Give My Regards to Broadway," "Yankee Doodle Dandy," and "You're a Grand Old Flag"? A. George M. Cohan

Q. Who is the only answer in the category "Brazilian Composers? A. Heitor Villa-Lobos

Q. This baroque instrument was similar to today's piano, with the notable exception that the strings were plucked rather than hit with hammers. A. Harpsichord

Q. This composer of the *German Requiem* is most famous for his lullaby. A. Johannes Brahms

Q. What "colorful" style of folk music for guitar, banjo, and violin is distinguished by rapid notes and improvisation by the musicians? A. Bluegrass

Q. What odd composer crammed all kinds of junk, bits of wood, weatherstripping, etc., into his "prepared pianos"? A. John Cage

Q. What instrument, called a licorice stick, was played by Benny Goodman? A. Clarinet

Q. Also called plainchant, the traditional music for Latin masses is this free-flowing rhythmic vocalization named for a pope. A. Gregorian chant

Q. What is the term for a gradual increase in the volume of a piece of music? A. Crescendo

Q. What American songwriter gave us the standards "Oh! Susanna," "Old Folks at Home," and "Beautiful Dreamer"? A. Stephen Foster

Q. What English duo created the operettas *HMS Pinafore, The Mikado,* and *The Pirates of Penzance?* A. Gilbert and Sullivan

Q. What Jewish, Russian-born composer gave us "White
Christmas" and "God Bless America"? *A.* Irving Berlin

MAJOR ART MOVEMENTS AND STYLES

Abstract Expressionism	U.S. founded, it emphasized spontaneous personal expression, often with artist becoming physically involved with painting, as by laying canvas on the floor and running across it, dripping and flinging paint. Jackson Pollock, Willem de Kooning major members.
Art Deco	1920s and '30s movement featuring sleek, curved lines and use of metals and modern materials.
Barbizon School	French landscape painters predating Impressionists, including Theodore Rousseau.
Baroque	Seventeenth- and eighteenth-century movement featuring violent movement, strong emotion, dramatic lighting and coloring. Rembrandt, Caravaggio, Bernini, and Reubens were proponents.
Cubism	Picasso and Braque's early twentieth-century movement featuring geometric fragmentation and multiple, simultaneous viewpoints.
Dadaism (or just Dada)	Movement of the 1920s in which artists reacted to horror of World War I with nonsensical antiart or nonart stressing the sense of absurdity they felt. Name supposedly chosen from dictionary at random and means "hobbyhorse" in French.
Fauvism	Early twentieth-century movement associated with Matisse featuring bright colors and spontaneous manner. Name means "wild beasts" in French.

Futurism	Italian movement with Marinetti and Boccioni glorifying modernity and the machine age in the 1930s.
Gothic	Generic term for art before the Renaissance, named for a barbarian tribe.
Impressionism	Mid-19th-century French movement focusing on transitory visual impressions and painting directly from nature. Name comes from *Impression: Sunrise* by Claude Monet. Includes Manet (he hated being called one), Degas, Renoir, Cassatt, Monet.
Op Art	Abstract art form focusing on optical illusions.
Pointillism	Style in which painting is built up of small dots, which blend together to produce final effect. George Seurat's *Sunday Afternoon on the Island of La Grand Jatte* is best example.
Rococo	Mainly French movement exemplified by Versailles and called Baroque gone mad. Features overly ornate, frilly, and elegant designs. Watteau and Fragonard.
Surrealism	Literally "super realism." Artists use extremely realistic-looking techniques to depict evocative, often disturbing glimpses into the psyche.

Art History in a Nutshell

One subject that comes up much more often than you might expect is art history. In my five games, I encountered two art history categories, three questions about art in other categories, and an art history question in Final Jeopardy! Fortunately, *Jeopardy!* tends to ask only about the major artists and movements, so you can bring yourself up to speed very quickly in this category. Let's begin with this list of fifteen art movements or styles that are asked about over and over again.

In virtually every *Jeopardy!* clue, the writers include a key phrase that can guide you to the response they are looking for. For example, if a question went on and on with obscure facts but then suddenly ended, "were all accomplished by this president and Supreme Court chief justice," you would be left with only William Howard Taft as an answer. I call these short phrases that apply to only one person "instant identifiers."

In Art history, these instant identifiers are usually an artist's distinctive subject or technique. So if a *Jeopardy!* clue contains the key words on the left in the list below, you should respond with the name on the right.

Instant Identifier	Artist
Soup cans	Andy Warhol
Flags or targets	Jasper Johns
Horses or ballet dancers	Edgar Degas
Babies and mothers	Mary Cassatt
Jewish village life	Marc Chagall
Flowery shapes and cowskulls	Georgia O'Keefe
Watercolor birds	John James Audubon
Peasants partying	Pieter Brueghel (the Elder)
Mobiles	Alexander Calder
English pastoral scenes	John Constable
Melting watches and swarming ants	Salvador Dalí
Nightclub dancers	Henri Toulouse-Lautrec
Brightly colored Polynesian women	Paul Gauguin
Self-portraits (many artists, but it's usually this guy)	Rembrandt
Revolutionary murals	Diego Rivera
Heartwarming small-town America	Norman Rockwell
Large, impressionistic bronze sculptures	Auguste Rodin
Voluptuous female nudes	Peter Paul Rubens

Swirling, expressionistic landscapes	Vincent van Gogh
Dutch domestic scenes	Jan Vermeer
Arrangements in Black and Gray or "his mother"	James Whistler
Plain-faced farm couple	Grant Wood
Geometric patterns in primary colors	Piet Mondrian
Bawdy English woodcuts that tell a story	William Hogarth
Portraits of Napoleon	Jacques David
Pictures of Napoleon's invasion of Spain	Francisco Goya
Religious subjects with distorted, elongated forms	El Greco
Watercolor of sailing and the sea	Winslow Homer
Realistic harsh scenes of urban life	Edward Hopper
Abstract paintings made by dripping and splashing paint	Jackson Pollock
Brightly colored sporting events	Leroy Neiman
Paintings that look like comic strips	Roy Lichtenstein
Sculptures made by wrapping huge area with cloth	Cristo

Answers to Quizzes

Answers to International Dance Quiz

1. Tango
2. Waltz
3. Quadrille
4. Reel
5. Mazurka
6. Fandango
7. Flamenco
8. Cancan
9. Cakewalk
10. Ballroom dances

CHAPTER 8

Cooking and Food

This category can be great fun to study for. I mean, what better way to study cooking and food than to eat good food and go to fine restaurants? *Jeopardy!* simply loves to ask about this very big subject.

SOURCES OF QUICK INFORMATION

The Frugal Gourmet. Jeff Smith. Avon Books, 1991. ISBN: 0380716798. The stuff he talks about just happens to be the same stuff that *Jeopardy!* asks about. *Joy of Cooking* simply has too much information.

Microsoft Encarta CD Encyclopedia. Using the find capabilities, read the sections on fruits and vegetables. You'll learn a ton.

COOKING TERMS AND EQUIPMENT

Jeopardy! loves to find out whether the contestants know their way around a kitchen. Below are questions about some of the more important cooking terms. How many can you get?

What's in That?

If you take your pie with ice cream, you have it "à la mode." Match each cooking term below with the food it tells you a dish includes.

Cooking Terms

1. À la russe
2. Florentine
3. Crécy

4. St.-Germain
5. DuBarry
6. Argenteuil

Foods

a. Asparagus
b. Cauliflower
c. Peas

d. Carrots
e. Spinach
f. Sour cream

Answers on page 126.

Q. To brighten the color of vegetables, try this, which means plunging them into boiling water for a few minutes. A. Blanching

Q. Though it sounds like something you'd do to a river bottom, in the kitchen it's rolling thinly sliced fish or meat in flour for frying or sautéeing A. Dredging

Q. If your carrots are shaped like matchsticks, they were cut this way. A. Julienne

Q. Hunting illegally or gently cooking fish, eggs, or meat in water at just below simmer. A. Poaching

Q. This cooking term is taken from the French word for "to jump." a. Sauté

Q. What does "looed" refer to in Chinese cooking? A. Simmering

Q. These are eggs set in melted butter, topped with cheese, pepper, and salt, and cooked in an oven for ten to fifteen minutes. A. Shirred eggs

Q. This very thin cut of veal comes from the center of the leg. A. Scallopini

Q. This name is shared by a salad dressing and a small decorative bottle for smelling salts. A. Vinaigrette

Q. This is a bottle or small dispenser for oil or vinegar used at the table. A. Cruet

Q. This small metal bowl has a handle that can be used when eating porridge. A. Porringer

Q. This six-letter word describes a broad, deep bowl used for serving soup. A. Tureen

A LITTLE DASH OF KNOWLEDGE: ALL ABOUT SPICES

Spices have been around for thousands of years and have played a remarkable role in the development of human culture. The extensive exploration of our planet that began in the 1400s was in large part motivated by a search for cheap and plentiful spices. Thus, it is no surprise that *Jeopardy!* frequently asks about them. Here are the essential facts to know, any of which could easily be a *Jeopardy!* question.

Q. This spice is essential to New England clam chowder—and a Simon and Garfunkel song. A. Thyme

Q. With the faith of a grain of this seed can you move biblical mountains. A. Mustard

Q. It's said to promote wisdom, and many cooks think turkey stuffing would be incomplete without it. A. Sage

Q. This yellow, expensive spice comes from Spain. A. Saffron

Q. Every kitchen should have on hand this blend of herbs and vegetables sautéed and used to flavor other dishes. A. Mirepoix

Q. This style of mustard comes from France. A. Dijon

Q. What country gives us five-spice powder? A. China

Q. What are the five spices in five-spice powder? A. Cinnamon, clove, fennel, anise, ginger

Q. Despite its name, this is not a blend of spices at all, but a single one. A. Allspice

Questions About Game Animals

Here's a category guaranteed to outrage vegetarians everywhere. Answer these questions about "game."

1. Civet de lapin is a french dish involving this animal.
2. Brunswick stew doesn't contain Brunswicks but often this arboreal rodent.
3. Chinese ringnecks and English ringnecks gave rise to what species of game bird?
4. Hungarian and chukar are two types of this small game bird.
5. What game bird is also sometimes known as a prairie chicken?
6. What is a bobwhite better known as?
7. What restaurants call a squab is actually a juvenile form of this.

Answers on page 126.

Q. This is an alternate name for a laurel leaf. A. Bay leaf

Q. This name is given to a bouquet of fresh herbs, including parsley, thyme, and bay leaves. A. Bouquet garni

Q. This rather sweet-flavored spice is common in Scandinavian and Middle Eastern cooking. A. Cardamom

Q. This mild French herb resembles parsley in flavor.
A. Chervil

Q. The fresh form of this is often called cilantro or Chinese parsley. A. Coriander

Q. In what nationality's cooking is cumin used a great deal?
A. Mexican

Q. What produces the special flavor in Italian sausage?
A. Fennel

Q. What candy's taste does fennel resemble? A. Licorice

Q. Ground sassafras leaves, it is essential in New Orleans cooking, especially gumbo. A. Filé

Q. This is a two-word name for a French blend of parsley, chervil, tarragon, and chives.   A. Fines herbes

Q. What herb does the Frugal Gourmet recommend you buy by the hand?   A. Ginger

Q. What spice comes from the outer covering of the nutmeg?   A. Mace

Q. What spice is derived from the dried stamens of a crocus?   A. Saffron

Q. What spice with a "delicious" name resembles thyme in flavor?   A. Savory

Q. What is the bitter, orange-colored spice that flavors pilafs, curry powders, and Indian braised dishes?   A. Turmeric

Q. This needle-shaped spice's name comes from the Latin for "dew of the sea."   A. Rosemary

Q. Although most people think of this flavoring as sold in "cloves," the biggest variety of it is called "elephant" size.   A. Garlic

A *JEOPARDY!* FAVORITE: SAUCES

The sauce can make the meal. On *Jeopardy!* your knowledge of sauces could make you some·serious money.

Q. This is the basic white sauce made of milk or stock and thickened with a roux.   A. Béchamel

Q. This northern Italian sauce contains basil, olive oil, garlic, cheese, and pine nuts.   A. Pesto

Q. Add dry sherry, Parmesan or Romano cheese, and Worchestershire sauce to a béchamel and get this sauce.   A. Mornay

Q. This French sauce blends egg yolks, lemon juice, butter, salt, mustard, and Tabasco.   A. Hollandaise

Q. Vinegar, red wine, beef stock, tarragon, pepper, and onions or shallots make this French sauce.   A. Bernaise

Q. Red wine, soup stock, mushrooms, shallots, butter, parsley, and cornstarch make this French sauce.   A. Bordelaise

Q. This Italian mayonnaise should contain plenty of garlic.
A. Aioli sauce

Q. Escoffier, the first famous chef, coined this term for the basic brown sauce not intending any reference to Spain.
A. Espagnole

Q. This sauce is what you get if you add tarragon and wine vinegar to a hollandaise sauce.   A. Bernaise

Q. This basic blend of oil or butter and flour is used to thicken gravies.   A. Roux

FROM AUBERGINE TO ZAARTAR: INTERNATIONAL CUISINE

Fine dining from around the world is one of the *Jeopardy!* writers' favorite categories. Here are some essential facts from French, Italian, Greek, Chinese, and other cuisines.

Q. This vegetable resembles Swiss chard but is lighter in color and flavor.   A. Bok choy

Q. This processed wheat is often used for Middle Eastern dishes.   A. Bulgur wheat

Q. These pickled buds are used in salads and dressings.
A. Capers

Q. Also called sai fun or glass noodles, they are made from the mung bean, not plastic.   A. Cellophane noodles

Q. What beans give us bean sprouts?   A. Mung beans

Q. This name is given to thinly sliced dough for Middle Eastern cooking.   A. Phyllo dough

Q. What salty liquid are grape leaves usually packed in?
A. Brine

Q. This is the soybean and pepper sauce common in Chinese recipes.   A. Hoisin sauce

Q. This very rich soybean jam is the remains of the process of making soy sauce.   A. Mein see

Q. What valley shares its name with another name for Chinese celery cabbage?   A. Napa

Q. This rice-shaped pasta is great for pilafs.   A. Orzo

Q. These expensive treasures are usually taken from Italian pinecones. A. Pine nuts

Q. This common kitchen chemical is used in corning beef or pork. A. Saltpeter

Q. This peanut-butter-like Middle Eastern paste is made of ground sesame seeds and sesame oil. A. Tahini

Q. This Lebanese blend of sumac bark, thyme, and chick-peas or sesame seeds is likely to be listed last in an alphabetical list of foods. A. Zaartar

Q. What common cooking ingredient might a Jewish grandmother call gildern yoich? A. Chicken stock

Q. This name is given to Italian hors d'oeuvres, which are served "before" the main course. A. Antipasto

Q. This is what the Spanish call hors d'oeuvres. A. Tapas

Q. This is what the Lebanese call hors d'oeuvres. A. Mezza

Q. What is the major ingredient in caponata, an Italian hors d'oeuvre? A. Eggplant

Q. What is the Jewish equivalent of a pancake? A. Latke

Q. What is the Russian version of a pancake? A. Blini

Q. Rosie Perez would have known this name for basically an egg and bacon pie. A. Quiche Lorraine

Q. This grain swells larger than any other grain. A. Barley

Q. What the marsala is in chicken marsala. A. Marsala wine

Q. This is a high-class Italian version of steak tartare. A. Carpaccio

Q. This taste delight is wrapped and rolled flank steak, eggs, garlic, and Swiss and Parmesan cheese, baked in an oven. A. Braciole

Q. What's the other name for hot beef shreds from China? A. Chungking shreds

Q. These are Greek meatballs. A. Youvarlakia

Q. This Greek dish is cubed lamb or pork, cooked in lemon juice and olive oil, on skewers. A. Souvlakia

Q. What national dish of Lebanon consists of ground, raw lamb made into a loaf and served on raw onions? A. Kibbe

Our Favorite Fungus—Much Ado About Mushrooms

1. What do the French call mushrooms?
2. What Japanese mushroom is similar to a Chinese black mushroom?
3. What romantic name is given to the most elegant of wild mushrooms?
4. What name is given to a tiny, slender, Japanese mushroom used in nouvelle cuisine as a garnish?
5. What is a dark-capped mushroom called?
6. What meteorological name is given to a Chinese black tree fungus?
7. Sometimes called a jelly mushroom, this Chinese mushroom is very fragile.
8. A garlic pine aroma indicates that these Japanese mushrooms are fresh.

Answers on page 127.

Q. This is a coarse meatloaf wherein the meat is cooked so long that it falls apart.   A. Rillette

Q. These are Mexican sausages.   A. Chorizo

Q. This "Food Beginning with the Letter Q" is a French meat or fish dumpling.   A. Quenelle

Q. What vegetable is called tartuffo by Spaniards, kartoffel by Germans, and kartofel by Russians?   A. Potato

Q. This is the onomatopoetic name for potatoes and cabbage cooked in a pan.   A. Bubble and squeak

Q. Italians often eat a whole one of these after a garlicky meal to cover their garlic breath.   A. Coffee bean

Q. This bacon and tripe soup was supposedly eaten by Washington at Valley Forge.   A. Pepper pot soup

Q. This Cajun stew contains sausages, ham, chicken, rice, and vegetables.   A. Jambalaya

Q. This North African dish consists of small, processed wheat balls. A. Couscous

Q. These are Chinese fermented black beans. A. Dow see

Q. This French canapé consists of mashed red peppers, garlic, potatoes, and bouillabaisse stock served on crackers. A. Rouille sauce

Q. This is the romantic-sounding French term for eggplant. A. Aubergine

Q. This French relish, whose name sounds like the sound of a tommy gun, derives from eggplants. A. Ratatouille

Q. These are the French equivalent of bouillon cubes. A. Glace de viande

Q. Cream cheese, sour cream, lemon juice, and sugar, mixed and formed in small teacups and served with berries. A. Hearts of crème

Q. The Greek name for flaming Greek cheese. A. Saganaki

Q. This is the name for baked Greek fish. A. Plaki

Q. This Greek garlic sauce is made with pieces of ground-up white bread. A. Skorthalia

Q. What is the key ingredient in Greece's melitzosalata dip? A. Eggplant

Q. This Greek salad is made from cucumbers and yogurt. A. Tzatziki

Q. This is what the Greeks call lasagna. A. Pastitso

Q. These Greek pillows of spinach and cheese take their name from "three feet." A. Tiropetakia

Q. These Jewish fish dumplings are often served at Passover. A. Gefilte fish

Q. This Jewish stuffed egg pancake is a frequent breakfast item. A. Blintze

Q. Apicius of Rome created the first known book of this type. A. Cookbook

Q. Garbanzo beans, tahini, garlic, and olive oil comprise this Middle Eastern spread. A. Hummus

Q. These Polish dough pockets can be stuffed with potatoes, cheese, or meat. A. Pierogi

Q. Sausage from this Polish city is what most of us think of as kielbasa. A. Krakow

Q. In French cooking, they are ground meat or vegetables mixed with cream sauce, dipped in batter, and deep fried. A. Croquettes

Q. This egg-based product is the key ingredient in oeufs à la neige. A. Custard

Q. To make one of them, take a light yeast cake and soak it in syrup of sugar water and dark rum. A. Baba au rhum or savarin

Q. New Orleans is famous for these fritters made of apples and other fruits, fried in butter. A. Beignets

Q. This cold Spanish soup is made with tomatoes, garlic, and shallots. A. Gazpacho

Food for Thought

Do you know the difference between Edam and Gouda cheese? How about which fish is called the "hippo of the sea"? The questions below are about the foods themselves and will take you through a full, multicourse meal from appetizers to the postprandial cup of Viennese coffee. Enjoy!

CHEESES AROUND THE WORLD

Man cannot live by bread alone; he must have some cheese. See what you know about the world's cheeses.

Q. What country gives us Kasseri cheese? A. Greece

Q. What cheese tops French onion soup? A. Swiss

Q. This blue goat-cheese from Italy has many international equivalents. A. Gorgonzola

Q. What French cheese most resembles Gorgonzola?
A. Roquefort

Q. Besides Parmesan or Romano, what kind of cheese is in a canneloni? A. Cottage

Q. What fruit is most associated with Bel Paese cheese?
A. Pears

Q. What American cheese is named for the rectangular shape it's served in? A. Brick

Q. What German cheese has caraway or anise in it?
A. Muenster

Q. This Canadian cheese is made from a secret Trappist monk recipe from France. A. Oka

Q. Golden dessert cheese from France, semisoft, ripened.
A. Pont l'Evéque

Q. This is the soft, ripened American version of Boursin, complete with white color and flecks of herbs. A. Alouette

Q. This yellow, soft, ripened cheese has an edible, thin brown-and-white crust. A. Brie

Q. This soft French cheese bought in foil wrappers should be slightly runny when just ripe. A. Camembert

Q. This is a strong-flavored American soft cheese with a German name. A. Liederkranz

Q. This very strong-odored Belgian or American cheese is said to be good with beer. A. Limburger

Q. Cheese that is sometimes called pot or farmer cheese.
A. Cottage cheese

Q. This Greek cheese is made from sheep's milk. A. Feta

Q. This is the most famous Norwegian cheese. A. Gjetost

Q. This mild unripened Italian cheese is a common addition to pizza. A. Mozzarella

Q. This white French cheese contains less fat than cream cheese and is used in lite cream cheese. A. Neufchâtel

Q. This Italian cheese is a lot like cottage cheese. A. Ricotta

Q. This Swiss cheese is hard, ripened, sharp, greenish.
A. Sapsago

Q. This piquant English cheese, which is milder than Roquefort, is the traditional cheese to accompany port.
A. Stilton

Q. This is Syrian firm, ripened cheese. A. Cashkavallo

Q. This Netherlands cheese is bought in cannonball shape, often in wax. A. Edam

Q. This Dutch cheese is bought in red wax coating with flattened top and bottom. A. Gouda

Q. This delicate French-Swiss cheese is used in cooking quiche Lorraine. A. Gruyère

Q. This mild to sharp American cheese is the one most frequently used in cooking. A. Monterey jack

Q. Noekkelost cheese is an orange breakfast cheese from what country? A. Norway

Q. What Italian cheese is bought in long pear shapes? A. Provolone

Q. What country gives us Emmenthal cheese? A. Switzerland

Q. Pale yellow with green specks, this cheese has a New England state's name in it. A. Vermont sage

THE ART OF THE SALAD

It's always a good idea to have a little greenery with your meal, so here are some questions about produce.

Q. These are the two key ingredients in a succotash. A. Corn and lima beans

Q. A classic part of French cuisine, it's a cross between an onion and garlic. A. Shallot

Q. Ceci, packed with nutrients and carbohydrates, also go by these two names. A. Garbanzo beans and chick-peas

Q. This type of cabbage has tightly packed crinkled leaves. A. Savoy

Q. This is the term for fermented and salted cabbage. A. Sauerkraut

Q. This salad green is made by replanting the roots of a decapitated chicory plant. A. Belgian endive

Q. This white-ribbed red cabbage is the Italian word for "chicory." A. Radicchio

Q. In 640 A.D., a Welsh army defeated a Saxon army in the British Isles, and the Welsh victory was credited partly to the fact that each Welsh soldier had affixed a certain vegetable to his helmet so that Welshmen would not accidentally kill Welshmen. What was this cousin to the onion, which now is the national emblem of Wales? A. Leek

Q. Onions belong to this family, which we usually associate with plants possessing a much better odor. A. Lilies

Q. What is the name for the fragile onion from Georgia? A. Vidalia

Q. What type of vegetable is a Walla Walla? A. Onion

ENTREE: SEAFOOD

Now we move to the main course. Let's have some seafood.

Q. This is the name for soft-shelled clams or early motor cars. A. Steamers

Q. What shellfish perished in "The Walrus and the Carpenter"? A. Oysters

Q. When salmon is "en gelée," it's in this. A. Gelatin

Q. Japan is not the only country featuring raw fish on the menu; Mexico offers this raw fish salad. A. Seviche

Q. What is put into an omelet in a Hangtown fry? A. Oysters

Q. Outside of what city was Hangtown? A. San Francisco

Q. French fishermen would throw everything they caught into a stew and call it this. A. Bouillabaisse

Q. This thicker soup results when bouillabaisse is strained and cream is added. A. Bisque

Q. This seafood can be cooked Provençale, Américaine, fricasse, or à la nage. A. Lobster

Q. This is lobster overbaked and stewed in the shell, or a month in the French Revolutionary calendar. A. Thermidor

Q. This is lobster stewed with creamy sauce, sherry, and legumes. A. Lobster Newburg

Q. Almost half of all crab eaten in the United States is of this variety. A. Snow crab

Q. This crab is found almost exclusively in the Pacific Northwest. A. Dungeness

Q. Jonah, peeky toe, and spider varieties of this shellfish can be found in Maine. A. Crab

Q. This type of crab is found in Florida waters. A. Stone crab

Q. The tanner variety of this shellfish is found in Southeast Asian waters. A. Crabs

Q. Most of the blue crabs eaten today are found in this bay. A. Chesapeake

Q. If you see this Japanese word on the menu, you are in for fake crab meat. A. Surimi

Q. A third of fillets and half of fish sticks are made from this fish. A. Cod

Q. This shellfish can move by propelling water with its shell; the muscle that does this is what we eat. A. Scallop

Q. This large flatfish is sometimes dubbed the "hippo of the sea." A. Halibut

Q. Possibly because they don't want to risk offending patrons, restaurateurs often use the term dorado to describe this fish. A. Dolphin

Q. This is added to a dish in Italy to make it tonnata. A. Tuna or tuna sauce

FRUIT: THE SENSIBLE DESSERT

Watch your weight and get some points. For dessert, answer these fruity questions.

Q. This fruit's two major types are freestone and clingstone. A. Peach

Q. This dessert consists of half a peach on vanilla ice cream with raspberry sauce poured over it all. A. Peach Melba

Q. Comice, Anjou, Winter Nellis, and Bosc are all types of this fruit. A. Pears

Q. This pumpkin-shaped melon is a major source of nutrition in the tropics. A. Casaba

Q. This is another name for fruits with pits in them.
A. Stone fruits

Q. Hachiya and fuyu are varieties of this fruit.   A. Persimmon

Q. This yellow, pear-shaped fruit contains enzymes that break down meat.   A. Papaya

Q. Another name for a carambola, which describes its shape.   A. Star fruit

Q. The Hawaiian solo variety of this fruit is best.   A. Papaya

AND FINALLY, AN AFTER-DINNER COFFEE

What better finish to a meal than a steaming cup of coffee? If you said "potent potable," see the next chapter. In the meantime, answer these questions about coffee.

Q. Add flamed cognac with sugar, spices, orange, and lemon rinds to black coffee and get this.   A. Cafe diablo or brulot

Q. This half espresso, half hot milk combination is often served with a cinnamon stick.   A. Cappuccino

Q. This flavorful root is widely used in the New Orleans area to flavor coffee.   A. Chicory

Q. Literally a "half cup," it is a small cup of coffee served after dinner.   A. Demitasse

Q. If you add whipped cream to strong black coffee you get this.   A. Viennese coffee

Q. Besides drunk, what you get if you add whiskey to coffee.
A. Irish coffee

Q. Mix ground coffee and sugar, add water, let it foam and settle, and repeat to make this.   A. Turkish coffee

Food Trivia

You might have known the questions above just from being a good cook or from frequently dining out, but the questions below are pure trivia. How many can you get?

Food Name Origins

Q. This food takes its name from the Latin for "cooking pot." A. Lasagna

Q. What food product takes its name from the Malay word for "taste"? A. Ketchup

Q. This frozen, flavored custard dessert is a "perfect" end to a French meal. A. Parfait

Q. Named for the root from which it is made, it's essential in 'smores. A. Marshmallow

Q. This word comes from the French word for any vegetable but now means specifically beans. A. Legume

Q. This dish is so named because it uses vegetables available in the spring. A. Pasta primavera

Q. The name of this Italian dish comes from the fact that the meat was first cooked over charcoal. A. Pasta carbonara

Q. This Italian way of preparing foods means "sharp," from the lemons and capers used in cooking the chicken or veal involved. A. Piccata

Q. This zucchini omelet from Italy is, as its name implies, fried. A. Frittata

Q. This is a loaf made of meat ground very fine, literally into a paste. A. Pâté

Q. This term originally refered to an animal roasted whole; now it refers mainly to the sauce meat is basted in.
A. Barbecue

Q. What dish takes its name from the American Indian dish misaquatash? A. Succotash

Q. This word literally means "sausage" in Polish. A. Kielbasa

Food and Geography

Jeopardy! loves to ask where foods come from or, better yet, about foods with places in their names. In the Tournament of Champions, for example, I was able to get "Jerusalem artichoke" simply because I wrote the following questions as preparation in the months leading up to the show.

Q. This member of the Sunflower family grown for its edible tubers is not an artichoke and is not from Israel; it gets its name from the word "Girasole" or sunflower. What is this misnamed vegetable? A. Jerusalem Artichoke

Q. With what southern city is Oysters Rockefeller associated? A. New Orleans

Q. What country gave us Caesar salad? A. Mexico

Q. Geographical name for thin slices of flank steak. A. London broil

Q. You might call these "Austrian franks." A. Vienna sausages

Q. This cold potato soup contains the name of a French resort city in its name. A. Vichyssoise

Q. This is a thin soup with beef or mutton and barley. A. Scotch broth

Q. This is a round steak, pounded, browned, and braised with gravy. A. Swiss steak

Q. It is cheese melted with beer and poured over toast. A. Welsh rarebit

Q. This southeastern province, whose name is often found in Chinese restaurant names, is the most famous farming region in China. A. Hunan

Q. It is a very hard brick of ice cream on sponge cake covered with meringue and baked. A. Baked Alaska

WHAT'S IN A NAME

Some foods have such silly names that *Jeopardy!* likes to make the contestants say them. "Ratatouille" is one of my favorites. I always feel like I'm imitating a machine gun when I say it. Whet your appetite on these questions about foods with interesting names.

Q. They're not an extreme weather condition; they are highly tender filets of beef cut from the tenderloin A. Tournedos

Q. It is a frothy white fudge with a heavenly name. A. Divinity fudge

Q. This beef-and-pâté dish is named for Arthur Wellesley.
A. Beef Wellington

Q. This Australian soprano has a dessert and a type of "toast"
named for her. A. Nellie Melba

Q. This meat can be served marengo, Kiev, or mole.
A. Chicken

Q. This term describes beef that has been pickled or preserved
in a salt solution. A. Corned beef

Q. Sartorial name for the New England mixture of chopped
corned beef, chopped cooked potatoes, chopped beets, and
seasonings served on an egg. A. Red flannel hash

Q. This animal is the hassen in hassenpfeffer; just ask Bugs.
A. Hare or rabbit

Q. Likened to angel hair, it is the thinnest of all pasta.
A. Capellini

Q. This is the three-word name for a Pennsylvania Dutch
apple desert. A. Apple pan dowdy

Q. What name is given to corn with the hull and germ
removed? A. Hominy

Answers to Quizzes

Answers to What's in That? Quiz

1. f	4. c
2. e	5. b
3. d	6. a

Answers to Questions About Game Animals Quiz

1. Rabbit	5. Grouse
2. Squirrel	6. Quail
3. Pheasant	7. Pigeon
4. Partridge	

Answers to Our Favorite Fungus—Much Ado About Mushrooms Quiz

1. Champignon
2. Japanese shiitake
3. Chanterelle
4. Enoki-dake
5. Morel
6. Cloud's ears
7. Straw mushroom
8. Shiitake

CHAPTER **9**

Science

This category can be hard to study for because there is so much obscure knowledge associated with it. *Jeopardy!* will only ask about the obvious stuff, though, so I have assembled the most important things that you need to know about science.

SOME LISTS TO MEMORIZE

Planets and their moons
Major constellations
Elements and their symbols
Major bones, organs, glands of the body
Lobes of the brain
Major kingdoms, phylums, and orders of the biological world (see
    pp. 55–68 in *The New York Public Library Desk Reference*, 2d ed.)

SOURCES OF QUICK INFORMATION

An Incomplete Education, chapter 11, "Science," p. 472–529
The Dictionary of Cultural Literacy, pp. 437–548

The Top 100 Facts in General Science

The key to learning science for *Jeopardy!* is knowing that they will only ask about the most important concepts. You will not be called upon to recite Schrödinger's wave equation, but you should know what a Geiger counter counts (radiation). Below, I have set out just the basic facts you need to know, without wasting your time with obscure material.

Q. Around −460° on the Fahrenheit scale, it is −273° on the Celsius scale and is the lowest possible temperature at which matter can exist. What is it? A. Absolute zero

Q. Velocity is the way we measure the change in position of an object over time, but what do we call the change in velocity of an object over time? A. Acceleration

Q. Technically, it's any substance that produces positive ions in solution; also, it's anything with a pH less than 7 and is the opposite of a base. What is it? A. Acid

Q. A right angle is one that is exactly 90 degrees, but what do we call one less than 90 degrees but more than 0? A. Acute

Q. What ancient science, which was obsessed with changing one metal into another, is considered the foundation of modern chemistry? A. Alchemy

Q. From the Arabic for "the broken bones," it is the branch of math in which letters or symbols are used to represent numbers. What is it? A. Algebra

Q. Lye and ammonia are two examples of bitter, caustic minerals of this variety. The "earth metals" on the left of the periodic table are also there. Name them. A. Alkalis

Q. Brass, steel, and pewter are examples of materials made up of two or more metals or of a metal and another material. What do we call them? A. Alloys

Q. In physics, the distance to the top of a wave crest or to the bottom of a wave trough is given what name? A. Amplitude

Q. Visible to the naked eye, this galaxy located near the constellation Pegasus is the closest one to the Milky Way.
A. Andromeda

Q. "I have found it" is what the Greek word "eureka" means
in English, and it is what this scientist screamed when he
figured out liquid displacement in a bathtub. Name him.
A. Archimedes

Q. The largest one of these bodies is Ceres, about 600 miles in
diameter, and the majority of them are found in a "belt"
between Mars and Jupiter. What are they?   A. Asteroids

Elemental Name Origins

Jeopardy! loves word origins and asks about them in any
category. Name the elements based on what their names mean.

1. Literally, the "new" element.

2. Watch out, Superman, it's the "hidden" element.

3. Marie Curie named this element, no. 84, for her native
   land, which isn't France.

4. Speaking of France, name the two elements named for
   France (one is based on the Roman name).

5. A noble gas, it is literally the "stranger."

6. Used in lightbulb filaments, its name means "heavy
   stone" in Swedish.

7. The lightest element, its name means "water former."

8. Elements 92, 93, and 94 are all named for planets. What
   are they?

9. Toughie: Name the only element named for a U.S. city.

10. Super Toughie: What Swedish city is the source of four el-
    emental names?

Answers on page 144.

Q. This type of positively charged particle, symbol α, is often produced by stripping a helium atom of its electrons, leaving two protons bound to two neutrons.   A. Alpha particle

Q. What word, from the Greek for "indestructible," denotes the smallest unit of an individual chemical element?
A. Atom

Q. The atomic weights in the periodic table are stated in proportion to the weight of what element, with atomic number 6?   A. Carbon

Q. Of mean, median, and mode, which one is determined by adding up all the values in a range and dividing by the number of values?   A. Mean

Q. In three-dimensional geometry, it is a straight line about which an object may rotate; there's one running from the North Pole to the South Pole. What is it?   A. Axis

Q. If you add a base to an acid you get water and one of these, such as NaCl. What is it?   A. Salt

Q. You will hit Polaris, the North Star, if you draw a line through the two "front" stars of what constellation?
A. Ursa Major/Big Dipper

Q. This Danish Nobel Prize–winning physicist contributed to the quantum theory of the atom; his son, Aage, also won the Nobel Prize.   A. Niels Bohr

Q. This unit of heat corresponds to that required to raise the temperature of one pound of water one degree Fahrenheit. Name this unit, often associated with air conditioners.
A. BTU (British Thermal Unit)

Q. What term refers to the force that causes an object to float when placed in a liquid?   A. Buoyancy

Q. What branch of mathematics deals with L'Hospital's Theorem, limits, and derivatives?   A. Calculus

Q. What is the amount of heat required to raise the temperature of a kilogram of water by one degree Celsius?
A. Calorie

Q. What are the thin vesels that connect veins and arteries in the body?   A. Capillaries

Q. In chemistry, what is a substance that causes a chemical reaction to occur but is not itself involved in the reaction?
A. Catalyst

Q. What name is given to the point in any solid where a single applied force could support it? A. Center of Gravity

Q. What is the apparent force that tends to move objects away from the center in a system in circular motion? A. Centrifugal force

Q. When the surfaces of two pieces of the same material stick together because of molecular attraction, what is it called? A. Cohesion

Q. Do the tails of comets always face away from the sun or toward it? A. Away

Q. What Polish scholar of the fifteenth to sixteenth century produced the first workable model of the solar system?
A. Nicholas Copernicus

Q. What name is given elementary particles, originating in the sun and other stars, that continuously rain down on the earth? A. Cosmic rays

Q. In what type of chemical bond do two atoms share some of their valence electrons, thereby creating a force that holds the atoms together? A. Covalent bonds

Q. In a nuclear reactor, what term is given to the amount of material that must be present before a chain reaction will occur? A. Critical mass

Q. What name is given to materials, such as glass, diamonds, or quartz, in which the atoms are arranged in a rigid geometrical structure marked by symmetry? A. Crystals

Q. What woman was the only person to win the Nobel Prize in two different sciences, physics and chemistry? A. Marie Curie

Q. What unit is used to measure the volume of sounds?
A. Decibels

Q. What physical property of a material is determined by dividing the mass of the material by its volume? A. Density

Q. What process, often associated with those with kidney ailments, refers to the separation of large and small molecules by diffusion through a membrane? A. Dialysis

Q. This process separates the constitutents of a liquid by boiling it and then condensing the vapor that results. A. Distillation

Q. What effect are we noticing when a moving automobile's horn sounds different when it's approaching us than when departing? A. Doppler effect

Q. In Einstein's equation $e = mc^2$, what does the c stand for? A. The speed of light

Q. In geometry, what is the curve traced out by a point that is required to move so that the sum of its distances from two fixed points (foci) remains constant? A. Ellipse

Q. What adjective is used to describe a chemical reaction in which heat is absorbed? A. Endothermic

Q. All isolated systems tend toward this, a measure of disorder. A. Entropy

Q. In physics, chemistry, and in the body, this "balanced" term describes a condition in which all influences acting cancel each other out so that a static situation results. A. Equilibrium

Q. Gasohol and alcoholic drinks contain what type of alcohol, produced by fermentation of sugars by yeast? A. Ethyl alcohol or ethanol

Q. What ancient Greek founded the study of geometry with his *Elements*? A. Euclid

Q. What temperature scale was devised by a German instrument maker in the eighteenth century? A. Fahrenheit

Q. What Italian-born American physicist built the first nuclear reactor, under the football field at the University of Chicago? A. Enrico Fermi

Q. In what process does a single large nucleus split into two or more smaller ones, releasing energy? A. Fission

Q. What is the emission of light from an object as a result of bombardment by outside energy sources? A. Fluorescence

Q. In physics, what is the number of crests of a wave that move past a given point in a given unit of time called? A. Frequency

Q. In a nuclear reactor, what is the combining of two small nuclei into a larger one, releasing energy? A. Fusion

Q. The collective name of the four largest moons of Jupiter salutes the scientist who discovered them. Who was it? A. Galileo

Q. Of the three common states of matter of earth, in which are the molecules moving the most? A. Gas

Q. What assistant to Ernest Rutherford invented a machine for detecting particles emitted by radioactive nuclei? A. Geiger

Q. What American scientist launched the first liquid-fuel rocket, in 1926? A. Robert Goddard

Q. What chemical element is composed of two protons, usually two neutrons, and usually two electrons? A. Helium

Q. In geometry and genetics, what term describes a three-dimensional spiral, resembling a spring? A. Helix

Q. In the "MHz" on your AM radio dial, the M is for "mega" and the Hz is the abbreviation for the international unit of frequency. What is its full name? A. Hertz

Q. What term, used to measure the power of engines, refers to the power equal to about 746 watts? A. Horsepower

Q. What American astronomer discovered that galaxies were all red-shifted, which means that the universe is expanding? A. Edwin Hubble

Q. The Hindenburg dirigible disaster in 1937 probably resulted from a spark igniting this highly flammable element with which the airship was filled. What was it? A. Hydrogen

Q. In geometry, what conic section is a pair of curves, each one having a single bend, with lines going on infinitely out from the bend? A. Hyperbola

Q. What name is given to the longest side of a right triangle? A. Hypotenuse

Q. In the experimental method, what is a statement of a possible explanation for some natural phenomenon, which is then tested for correctness?
A. Hypothesis

Q. In physics, what is the tendency for objects at rest to remain at rest, and for objects in motion to continue so unless acted upon by an outside force? A. Inertia

Q. What is the name for radiation with wavelengths just longer than those of visible light? A. Infrared

Q. What is the collective term for all positive and negative whole numbers and zero? A. Integers

Q. What do we call the disturbance that occurs when two waves come together at a single point in space?
A. Interference

Q. What is an atom that has either lost or gained one or more electrons so that it has an electric charge? A. Ion

Q. What do mathematicians call a number, like pi, that cannot be expressed as the ratio of two whole numbers?
A. Irrational

Q. In chemistry, what are molecules that contain the same numbers of the same kinds of atoms in different arrangements? A. Isomers

Q. In chemistry, what do we call forms of the same element with different numbers of neutrons? A. Isotopes

Q. What English lord, one of the founders of thermodynamics, was born William Thompson? A. Lord Kelvin

Q. Whose first law states that the orbits of the planets are ellipses? A. Kepler

Q. What term, starting with K, denotes the energy an object has because of its motion? A. Kinetic energy

Q. Whether he discovered oxygen or not, what Frenchman is credited with giving oxygen its name?
A. Antoine Lavoisier

Q. Okay, which is which? Does an acid turn red litmus paper blue or blue litmus paper red? A. Blue to red

Q. What "number" is the speed of an object measured in multiples of the speed of sound, often applied to jets?
A. Mach number

Q. Of mean, median, or mode, which is the point in a range of values at which half the values will fall below it and half will fall above it? A. Median

Q. What Russian chemist is credited with devising the modern version of the periodic table? A. Dmitri Mendeleyev

Q. Of mean, median, and mode, which one means the most frequently appearing value in a set of values? A. Mode

Q. Horsehead, Lagoon, Dumbell, North America—all of these are names of what hazy clouds of interstellar gas, which are often formed by exploding stars? A. Nebulae (the singular is nebula)

Q. Oddly, the name of one of the final stages of a star, when it expands to many times its original size, means "new" in Latin. What is it? A. Nova

Q. What branch of physics deals with light and its properties? A. Optics

Q. What branch of chemistry deals with molecules consisting of carbon in long chains or rings, bonded with nitrogen, oxygen, or hydrogen? A. Organic chemistry

Q. What is the seeping of a fluid through a semipermeable membrane such as the cell wall? A. Osmosis

Q. What conic section consists of the set of points equidistant from a line, called a directrix, and a point, called a focus? A. Parabola

Q. What scientist, who advocated Vitamin C to ward off illness, won the Nobel Prize in chemistry and in peace? A. Linus Pauling

Q. What is the point in the orbit of a satellite at which it is closest to the earth? A. Perigee

Q. What is pH an abbreviation for? A. Potential of hydrogen

Q. What is the quantum, or bundle of energy, in which light is emitted called? A. Photon

Nuclear Physics in a Nutshell

Remember how I said that *Jeopardy!* loves to make easy questions look hard? Well, they also like to ask questions in tough-sounding categories whose names will intimidate the average viewer. Nuclear physics is a perfect example. It will make an impressive category name, but *Jeopardy!* will only ask the most basic information about it. Here are those most basic facts:

- The center of an atom is a nucleus.
- Orbiting the nucleus are lightweight particles called electrons.
- Inside the nucleus are heavy particles called hadrons (meaning "heavy").
- The two types of hadrons are protons and neutrons.
- Protons have a positive charge, electrons a negative one, and neutrons none.
- Certain particles with a "medium" weight are called mesons.
- Three quarks make up each of the hadrons. Electrons are not made of quarks.
- Quarks take their name from *Finnegans Wake* by James Joyce, which includes the line "Three quarks for Muster Mark!" They come in two "flavors"—"up" and "down"—in several "colors," and in such varieties as "top," "bottom," "strange," "charm," and "beauty." All those words are just terms, not real attributes of quarks.
- Gluons hold together the particles in the nucleus.
- Photons are the particles that carry light.
- Four forces hold the universe together: the strong, weak, electrostatic, and gravitational forces. Scientists are looking for a Grand Unification Theory, which would show that all the forces are really just one force.
- Scientists have linked the electrostatic and weak forces.

Q. What name is given to a solid material that is formed in a solution by chemical reactions and settles on the bottom of the container? *A.* Precipitate

Q. What name is given to rapidly rotating neutron stars? *A.* Pulsars

Q. What elementary particles make up electrons, protons, and neutrons? *A.* Quarks

Q. What term describes the change in direction that light undergoes when it enters a medium with a different density? *A.* Refraction

Q. What man discovered the existence of atomic nuclei by bombarding gold foil with alpha particles until one bounced back? *A.* Ernest Rutherford

Q. Literally meaning "sun stands still," what do we call the two occasions in the year when the sun stops getting either higher or lower in the sky? *A.* Solstice

Q. What is a four-sided polygon in which two sides are parallel and two are not? *A.* Trapezoid

Q. With an atomic weight of 92, what is the heaviest naturally occurring element? *A.* Uranium

Q. In mathematics and physics, what term is used to describe a quantity with both direction and magnitude, such as velocity? *A.* Vector

Q. What term describes a fluid's internal resistance to flow? *A.* Viscosity

Q. Named for an eighteenth-century Scottish inventor, what is the unit for power? *A.* Watt

GROSS ANATOMY, *JEOPARDY!* STYLE

You don't have to go to medical school to do well on the human body questions that *Jeopardy!* asks. All you have to do is read this quiz.

Q. What is the largest cranial bone? *A.* Parietal bone

Q. What cranial bone is the one closest to the spinal cord? *A.* Occipital bone

Q. What is another name for the breastbone? A. Sternum

Q. What is another name for the shinbone? A. Tibia

Q. Some car seats have supports for what lowest type of vertebrae? A. Lumbar

Q. What name, from the Latin for "neck," is given to the top set of vertebrae? A. Cervical

Q. What are the small bones in your hand, between the carpals and the phalanges, called? A. Metacarpals

Q. What are the small bones in your foot, between the tarsals and the toes, called? A. Metatarsals

Q. Though this is the generic term for any body cavity, or channel, most of us associate the term with the passages in our face that might get swollen and sore. A. Sinus

Q. What term means relating to the front or lower surface of a body? A. Ventral

Q. What is the term for a bone of very small size, such as those in the inner ear? A. Ossicle

Q. What are in trouble if you suffer from caries? A. Teeth

Q. What is the term for a hole of passageway in a bone? The "magnum" one your spine passes through is the most noted. A. Foramen

Q. What are the bands or strips of fibrous tissue connecting moving bones or cartilages called? A. Ligaments

Q. What small region at the end of the medulla oblongata serves as the "bridge" to the brain? A. Pons

Q. What is the "small brain" area located under the occipital lobe that controls balance and coordination? A. Cerebellum

Q. What term is given to the figure of a man with each body proportion part drawn in proportion to the area of the brain used to control it? A. Homunculus

Q. What are the membranes surrounding the brain and spinal column called? A. Meninges

Q. What name is given to the area in the center of the brain above the hypothalamus but below the gray matter? A. Corpus callosum

Q. What is the Latin name for the shoulder blade?
A. Scapula

Q. What two large veins bring blood back to the heart from the upper and lower body extremities? A. Vena cava

Q. What name is given to each branch of the trachea?
A. Bronchus (the plural is bronchi)

Q. The parotid, submaxillary, and sublingual glands produce what aid to digestion? A. Saliva

Q. What five-letter word describes food that is being acted upon in the stomach? A. Chyme

Q. The duodenum, jejunum, and ileum are three sections of what body part? A. Small intestine

Q. What organ is the largest internal organ? A. Liver

Q. What small organ stores and concentrates the bile and sends it into the small intestine? A. Gallbladder

Q. What largest part of the brain, located up front, controls voluntary muscles, intelligence, and emotions?
A. Cerebrum

Q. What do we call the mini-brain located behind and below the cerebrum? A. Cerebellum

Q. The cover of the brain is given what two-word name?
A. Cerebral cortex

Q. Located in the throat, what gland regulates the rate of metabolism? A. Thyroid

Q. What ducts lead from the kidneys to the bladder?
A. Ureters

Q. What duct carries urine out of the bladder and away from the body? A. Urethra

Q. A lack of niacin will cause what disease? A. Pellagra

Q. A deficiency of what vitamin will cause beriberi?
A. Vitamin B_1 (thiamine)

Q. A lack of folic acid or iron will cause what deficiency?
A. Anemia

Q. Pernicious anemia is caused by a lack of what B vitamin?
A. Vitamin B_{12}

Q. What vitamin is essential to blood clotting? A. Vitamin K

Q. Rickets results from a lack of what vitamin, produced by sunshine? A. Vitamin D

Q. Trace amounts of what mineral, Mg on the periodic table, have been shown to help transmission of electrical impulses in the body? A. Magnesium

Q. What Greco-Roman physician is seen as the founder of the "modern" rational, as opposed to superstitious, school of medicine? A. Galen

Q. What British doctor discovered the circulation of blood? A. William Harvey

Q. Using the newly invented microscope, what man discovered cells in the seventeenth century? A. Robert Hooke

Q. What Brit pioneered the use of inoculation, particularly against smallpox? A. Edward Jenner

Q. Tuberculosis was figured out by what German microbiologist? A. Robert Koch

Q. Who used the microscope—which he's sometimes credited with inventing—to discover bacteria? A. Anton van Leeuwenhoek

Q. Antiseptic surgery was the brainchild of what Brit? A. Joseph Lister

Q. What sixteenth-century Italian undertook in-depth study of human anatomy? A. Andreas Vesalius

Q. August von Wasserman discovered a test for what veneral disease? A. Syphilis

Q. What two arteries are located on either side of the neck and supply the brain with oxygen? A. Carotid arteries

Q. The gallbladder is located directly underneath what large organ? A. Liver

Q. What large muscle in your thigh is the longest in your body? A. Sartorius

Q. the gastrocnemius is the muscle which makes up what part of your leg? A. Calf

Q. The maxilla bone in your face works in opposition with what bone, also called the jawbone? A. Mandible

Q. What is the cranial bone located just above your ear called? A. Temporal bone

Q. What protein found in blood serum, milk, and egg whites takes its name from the Latin for "white"? A. Albumen

Q. What term, meaning "small body" in Latin, refers to any free-moving blood cell? A. Corpuscle

Q. What is the scientific term for a red blood cell? A. Erythrocyte

Q. The gamma variety of what protein, often an antibody, helps immunity? A. Globulin

Q. This substance on the surface of red blood cells reacts adversely to cells lacking it. A. Rh factor

Q. The hemoglobin molecule is based on this element. A. Iron

Q. This term refers to a blood clot that is drifting in the bloodstream A. Embolus

Q. This term refers to a fixed blood clot in a vessel or the heart. A. Thrombus

Q. This small blood-purifying organ is located below the stomach. A. Spleen

Q. This "-otomy" refers to the practice of bloodletting by opening a vein. A. Phlebotomy

Q. This six-letter verb starting with w means to become soaked in or covered with blood. A. Welter

Q. This seven-letter verb means to check or stop the flow of blood. A. Staunch

Q. Caisson disease is another name for this pressure-related condition often suffered by divers. A. The bends or nitrogen narcosis

Q. Heart attack victims often suffer a myocardial one of these, meaning dead tissue caused by a blood clot. A. Infarction

Q. This term describes any network of nerves and blood vessels, or part of Henry Miller's *Rosy Crucifixion* trilogy. A. Plexus

Q. This is the term for a sac, bulge, or pouch in the weakened wall of a blood vessel. A. Aneurysm

Major Inventions and Their Discoverers

Subatomic Particles

Electron	J. J. Thompson
Neutron	James Chadwick
Proton	Ernest Rutherford
Meson	Hideki Yukawa (he wanted to name it a "yukon")
Quarks	Murray Gell-Mann and George Zweig

Chemistry

Sodium, potassium, and many other elements	Sir Humphry Davy
Oxygen	Joseph Priestly
Periodic table	Dmitri Mendeleyev
Spectroscopic analysis	Bunsen and Kirchoff
Radium and polonium	Pierre and Marie Curie

Biology, Anatomy, and Medicine

That electrical impulses stimulate muscles	Luigi Galvani
Circulation of blood	William Harvey
Double helix structure of DNA	Watson, Crick, and Wilkins
Speech center of the brain	Pierre Broca (as in Broca's Brain)
Insulin-secreting cells in pancreas	Karl Langerhans
X rays	William Roentgen
Polio vaccine	Jonas Salk
Oral polio vaccine	Albert Sabin
Biological classification	Carolus Linnaeus
Theory of natural selection	Charles Darwin
Theory of genetics	Gregor Mendel
Human heart transplant	Christiaan Barnard
Penicillin	Alexander Fleming

Inventions

Telephone	Alexander Graham Bell
Bifocals	Benjamin Franklin
Dynamite	Alfred Nobel

Cyclotron	Ernest O. Lawrence
Barometer	Torricelli
Mercury thermometer	Gabriel Fahrenheit
Lightning Rod	Benjamin Franklin
Cotton gin	Eli Whitney
Elevator	James Otis
Frozen Food	Clarence Birdseye
Kodak (first hand-held) camera	George Eastman
AC motor	Nikola Tesla
Railway brake	George Westinghouse

Astronomy

Uranus	William Herschel
Neptune	Adams and Leverrier
Pluto	predicted by Percival Lowell found by Clyde Tombaugh
Laws of planetary motion	Johannes Kepler
Theory of gravity	Isaac Newton
Law that all galaxies are moving apart	Hubble's law
Biggest moons of Jupiter	Galileo
Radiation belts around Earth	James Van Allen
Liquid-fueled rocket	Robert Goddard

Answers to Quizzes

Answers to Elemental Name Origins Quiz

1. Neon
2. Krypton (not Kryptonite, by the way)
3. Polonium (for Poland)
4. Francium and Gallium (Lutetium, no. 71, is from the Roman name for Paris)
5. Xenon
6. Tungsten
7. Hydrogen
8. Uranium, Neptunium, Plutonium
9. Berkelium, named for Berkeley, California
10. Ytterby, Sweden (Ytterbium, Yttrium, Terbium, Erbium)

CHAPTER 10

History

SOME LISTS TO MEMORIZE

Presidents: Candidates, vice-presidents, doctrines, cabinets
Battles of the Revolutionary War, the Civil War, WWI, and
   WWII
Constitutional amendments
Order of succession to the presidency

GENERAL AMERICAN HISTORY

I wrote the very first question in this section, about Washington
crossing the Delaware, while I was preparing to go on my first
five shows. A question almost exactly like it appeared as a Daily
Double in my fifth game. It was almost word-for-word the same
as mine. Unfortunately, one of my opponents had picked that
Daily Double. Still, it just goes to show how writing questions
and watching the show really can get you to think like a *Jeopardy!*
writer.

Q. George Washington crossed the Delaware to fight and win
   this battle. *A.* Battle of Trenton

Q. In 1785, this state chartered the first state university.
A. Georgia
Q. In 1790, Pope Pius VI made him the first Catholic bishop in the United States.   A. John Carroll
Q. Indians of what future state were defeated at the Battle of Fallen Timbers?   A. Ohio
Q. In 1803, a federal outpost was founded at Fort Dearborn, future site of this city.   A. Chicago.

Presidential Nicknames

One of the most frequent categories is "Presidents," so this chapter has lots of material on them. You should know this stuff cold before stepping on the set.

Father of Our Country	George Washington
Old Rough and Ready	Zachary Taylor
Little Magician; Old Kinderhook	Martin Van Buren
The Dark Horse President	James Polk
The Sage of Monticello	Thomas Jefferson
The Sage of Hyde Park	Franklin Roosevelt
The Red Fox	Thomas Jefferson (he had red hair)
Handsome Frank	Franklin Pierce
The Sage of Campobello	Franklin Roosevelt

Q. The U.S. received land in this future state via the Adams-Onis Treaty of 1819.   A. Florida
Q. Presidential candidate John Quincy Adams promised this man the secretary of state position in return for his vote in the so-called corrupt bargain.   A. Henry Clay
Q. What the South called the tariff of 1828.   A. Tariff of Abominations
Q. This church was founded in Fayette, New York, in 1830.
A. The Church of Jesus Christ of Latter-Day Saints (i.e., the Mormons)

Q. This was the first law "nullified" by South Carolina.
A. Tariff of Abominations
Q. This party was formed by Daniel Webster and Henry Clay. A. Whigs
Q. In 1835, he survived the first attempt to assassinate a president. A. Andrew Jackson.

Presidential Homes

Mount Vernon	George Washington
Monticello	Thomas Jefferson
Hyde Park	Franklin Roosevelt
Sagamore Hill	Theodore Roosevelt
Kinderhook, N.Y.	Martin Van Buren
Hermitage	Andrew Jackson
Ash Lawn	James Monroe
Wheatlands, in Penn.	James Buchanan
Hyannisport	John F. Kennedy
Rancho Cielo	Ronald Reagan
San Clemente	Richard Nixon
Walker's Point	George Bush
Montpelier	James Madison

Q. This 1847 legislation, which forbade the expansion of slavery, panicked the South. A. Wilmot Proviso
Q. In this document, the U.S. threatened to seize Cuba.
A. Ostend Manifesto
Q. In 1856, the first Republican presidential convention picked this man for candidate. A. John C. Frémont
Q. In 1867, farmers organized the Patrons of Husbandry, a precursor to this movement. A. Grange
Q. The Burlingame Treaty allowed immigration from this country. A. China
Q. The Public Credit Act promised repayment of federal debts in this currency. A. Gold

Q. This lode was discovered in Nevada in 1859. A. Comstock Lode

Q. Congress enacted the first federal income tax to pay for the expenses of this war. A. Civil War

Q. Robert E. Lee's Confederate army was crippled in this campaign of 1864. A. Wilderness Campaign

Q. The Sand Creek Massacre of the Arapaho and Cheyenne Indians occurred in this western state. A. Colorado

Q. This organization was founded by Union veterans in 1865. A. Grand Army of the Republic

Q. This scandal in 1872 implicated Vice President Schuyler Colfax and embarrassed President Grant. A. Credit Mobilier Scandal

Q. Before 1933, and this amendment, the president was inaugurated on March 4. A. 20th Amendment

Q. Women voted for the first time in 1920, after this amendment was ratified. A. 19th Amendment

Q. This state had more signers of the Constitution than any other. A. Pennsylvania

Q. The initial name for them, Russellites, is derived from the name of their founder, Charles Taze Russell. A. Jehovah's Witnesses

Q. In 1874, this movement began bringing educational speakers to rural communities all over the nation. A. Chautauqua

Q. In 1875, Aristides became the first winner of this horse race. A. Kentucky Derby

Q. He opened his first five-and-dime store in Lancaster, Pennsylvania, in 1879. A. F. W. Woolworth

Q. In 1883, this "Queen City" was drowned by a flooding Ohio River. A. Cincinnati

Q. Distinction of the Home Insurance building in Chicago, Illinois, built in 1884. A. Considered the first skyscraper

TWENTIETH CENTURY POP HISTORY

The single most important category on the show is this one. In fact, it is practically a definition of the show. This is especially true since the 1997–98 season began, for the writers seem to be focusing a little more on entertainment and pop culture. Because of that, I have devoted several pages to just this period of our cultural history.

Q. What word game was invented by Alfred Butts and formerly called Criss-Cross? A. Scrabble

Q. What secretary of labor under FDR was the first woman in the cabinet? A. Frances Perkins

Q. What name did FDR give to his series of famous 1933 radio addresses? A. Fireside Chats

Q. The first worldwide radio broadcast covered what English king's coronation? A. George VI

Q. "Oh, the humanity!" cried Herbert Morrison as he covered what tragic event for nationwide audiences at Lakehurst, New Jersey, in 1937? A. *Hindenberg* disaster

Q. The Daughters of the American Revolution excluded what African-American opera star from performing at Constitution Hall? A. Marian Anderson

Q. Hungarian-American inventor and CBS engineer Peter Goldmark added what feature to TV in the 1950s?
A. Color

Q. What "timely" company had the first TV ads? A. Bulova watches

Q. What is the name of the wife of Dagwood Bumstead?
A. Blondie

Q. What museum was formerly called the Museum of Nonobjective Painting? A. Guggenheim Museum

Q. Louis Reard made a big splash when he designed what article of clothing named for a Pacific atoll? A. Bikini

Q. What company made a cheap, reliable TV in the 1940s and '50s that was dubbed the "Model T of TV"? A. RCA

Q. What troubled inventor devised the Polaroid camera?
A. Edwin Land
Q. NBC's *Television Theatre* was sponsored by what food company? A. Kraft.

Presidential Quick Facts

Pre-Presidency Employment

Ran a haberdashery	Harry Truman
Sheriff of Buffalo, New York	Grover Cleveland
Commander of PT 109	John F. Kennedy
Apprenticed to a tailor	Andrew Johnson
Peanut farmer	Jimmy Carter
Civil engineer	Herbert Hoover
Oil Tycoon	George Bush

Post-Presidency Employment

Confederate congressman	John Tyler
Massachusetts congressman	John Quincy Adams
Tennessee congresssman	Andrew Johnson
Supreme Court chief justice	William H. Taft

Q. What man hosted the *Original Amateur Hour?* A. Ted Mack
Q. What man's Actors Studio provided training in method acting? A. Lee Strasberg
Q. What was the first made-for-TV cartoon? A. *Crusader Rabbit*
Q. What was the first late-night variety show? A. *Broadway Open House*
Q. In 1950, this became the first Credit Card. A. Diner's Club
Q. The Census Bureau began using this first computer in 1951. A. UNIVAC
Q. This former radio show had TV's first all-black cast.
A. *Amos 'n' Andy*

Q. Network with the "unblinking eye." A. CBS

Q. Television viewers were enthralled to watch this mobster testify before the Senate in 1951. A. Frank Costello

Q. This daily variety show host had a hit with *House Party*. A. Art Linkletter

Q. He was the first *Today Show* host. A. Dave Garroway

Q. She/he became an instant international scandal by undergoing a sex change. A. Christine Jorgenson

Q. This baby was on the first *TV Guide*. A. Desi Arnaz Jr.

Q. This film process premiered in *The Robe*. A. Cinemascope

Q. Host of CBS's *See It Now*. A. Edward R. Murrow

Q. Turn-of-the-century consumer-oriented camera. A. Brownie Box

Q. This 1900s hottest dance craze involved a dessert. A. Cakewalk

Q. He wrote *Up From Slavery*. A. Booker T. Washington

Q. In 1904 a German, Richard Sterb, invented this toy with a presidentially inspired name. A. Teddy bear

Q. This jazz pianist penned "The King Porter Stomp." A. Jelly Roll Morton

Q. True to their name, these French brothers made the first color film. A. Lumière

Q. Distinction in film history of Gertie the Dinosaur. A. First cartoon

Q. Discoverer of the North Pole. A. Robert Peary

Q. William D. Boyce founded the American branch of this youth organization. A. Boy Scouts

Q. "Alexander's Ragtime Band" was composed by this man. A. Irving Berlin

Q. This city is mentioned in the first blues song. A. Memphis ("Memphis Blues")

Q. This addictive pastime debuted in 1914 in the *NY World*. A. Crossword

Q. She wrote *Family Limitation* in 1915. A. Margaret Sanger

Q. She starred in *Merchant of Venice* in 1915, with a wooden leg. A. Sarah Bernhardt

Q. This Massachusetts theater group is associated with the plays of Eugene O'Neill. A. Provincetown Players

Q. First jazz record in the U.S. A. "Dixie Jazz Band One-Step"

Q. Boxer called the Manassa Mauler. A. Jack Dempsey

Q. Hercule Poirot first appeared in this Agatha Christie novel. A. *Mysterious Affair at Styles*

Q. This station in Pittsburgh was the first radio station. A. KDKA

Q. Margaret Gorman, in 1921, was the first to win this title. A. Miss America

Q. This orchestra leader was the first to have a million-selling record with his "whispering." A. Paul Whiteman

Q. He represented Leopold and Loeb, among other pariahs. A. Clarence Darrow

Q. Harold Gray created her. A. Little Orphan Annie

Q. Founder of the *New Yorker*. A. Harold Ross

Q. Male and female symbols of the *New Yorker*. A. Eustace and Eustacia Tilly

Q. What *The WSM Barn Dance* grew up to be. A. *The Grand Ole Opry*

Q. It was introduced the third Sunday in April 1918 at 2:00 A.M. A. Daylight Savings Time

Q. "Lolly Willowes" was its first selection, for January 1926. A. Book-of-the-Month Club

Q. This film legend presented the first Oscars. A. Douglas Fairbanks Sr.

Q. Founder of CBS. A. William Paley

Q. Leader of RCA when it introduced color TV. A. David Sarnoff

Q. October 24, 1929, is known as this. A. Black Thursday

Q. Museum founded by an heir to the Vanderbilt fortune. A. Whitney Museum

Q. First *Tonight Show* host. A. Steve Allen

Q. This company debuted the TV dinner. A. Swanson

Q. This segment of the Disneyland hour set off a national craze for a certain type of cap. A. Davy Crockett

Q. Sam Phillips was the head of this record company. A. Sun Records

Q. In 1957, he was the conductor of the New York Philharmonic. A. Leonard Bernstein

Q. First TV show with black host. A. *Nat King Cole Show*

Q. Toy company founded by Ruth and Elliot Handler. A. Mattel

Q. Longest running Off-Broadway show in history. A. *The Fantasticks*

Q. Literally "no egg," it was the name of the first birth control pill. A. Enovid

Q. In 1961 she sang *Il Trovatore* and got a forty-five-minute standing ovation. A. Leontyne Price

Q. Longtime host of *Wide World of Sports*. A. Jim McKay

Q. First American in space. A. Alan Shepard

Q. This 1962 western was the first series to air ninety-minute episodes. A. *The Virginian*

Q. This Canadian published *Understanding Media* in 1964. A. Marshall McLuhan

Q. This Grace Metalious work became the first primetime soap. A. *Peyton Place*

Q. He was Hasbro's hottest hit in 1964. A. GI Joe

Q. He asked youngsters to send cash from Dad's wallet. A. Soupy Sales

Q. They were the first girl group to top the *Billboard* album chart. A. Supremes

Q. Sandoz Pharmaceuticals first marketed this drug. A. LSD

Q. They were the two founders of the Black Panthers. A. Huey Newton and Bobby Seale

Q. Singer who died in plane crash in 1967. A. Otis Redding

Q. 1966 California International Pop Festival. A. Monterrey

Q. 21-year-old founder of *Rolling Stone*. A. Jann Wenner

Q. President who established PBS. A. LBJ

Q. Considered the first "spaghetti western." *A. A Fistful of Dollars*

Q. Director of first spaghetti western. *A.* Sergio Leone

Q. In 1967, this nonfiction book (not the Bible) was the best-selling book in the world. *A.* Mao's little red book, *Quotations From Chairman Mao*

Q. David Crosby's song "A Long Time Coming" is about his 1968 assassination. *A.* RFK

Q. Candidate who was on *Laugh-in*. *A.* Richard Nixon

Q. She became one of the earliest African-American stars on TV, with *Julia*. *A.* Diahann Carroll

Q. They were the first two *60 Minutes* guys. *A.* Mike Wallace, Harry Reasoner

Q. Singer who was arrested in 1969 for lewd and lascivious conduct, while onstage. *A.* Jim Morrison

Q. John and Yoko were married on this "rocky" British territory. *A.* Gibraltar

Q. This was the infamous site of the Rolling Stones concert where Hell's Angels, hired as security guards, beat a man to death while the band performed. *A.* Altamont

Q. Tiny Tim married her on national TV. *A.* Miss Vickie

Q. Fillmore East and West musicians are associated with him. *A.* Bill Graham

Q. The first celebrity fundraiser was for this country. *A.* Bangladesh

Q. Rocker who died in 1970 motorcycle accident. *A.* Duane Allman

Q. In 1972, she founded *Ms*. *A.* Gloria Steinem

Q. Indian who accepted Marlon Brando's Oscar. *A.* Sasheen Littlefeather

Q. Conductor of the Boston Symphony. *A.* Seiji Ozawa

Q. TV movie with Cicely Tyson (besides *Roots*). *A. Autobiography of Miss Jane Pittman*

Q. She was on the first cover of *People* magazine. *A.* Mia Farrow

Q. She was a lab worker at a Kerr-McGee plutonium plant.
A. Karen Silkwood

Q. He was the first *Saturday Night Live* guest host. A. George Carlin

Q. The first TV miniseries, in 1976, it had Strauss, Blakely, and Nolte as its stars. A. *Rich Man, Poor Man*

Q. This aunt of Prince Charles was once married to Lord Snowden. A. Princess Margaret

Q. First openly gay TV character was on *Soap* and played by this man. A. Billy Crystal

Q. She was the first test tube baby. A. Louise Brown

Q. The leader caused mass suicide in the Jonestown tragedy.
A. Jim Jones

Q. This news show began as an ABC series covering the hostages in Iran. A. *Nightline*

Q. He was the most famous patient in Utah in 1982.
A. Barney Clark

Q. 1984's Mayflower Madam, she has written a book on how to keep your husband at home. A. Sidney Biddle Barrows

Q. This group had the first gold rap album. A. Run DMC

Q. When they got together to save the children, this was Band Aid's song. A. "Do They Know It's Christmas?"

Q. She is the famous wife of Edwin Schlossberg. A. Caroline Kennedy

Q. Prince Andrew married this redhead. A. Sarah Ferguson

Q. *A.M. Chicago* became this huge show. A. *Oprah*

Q. In front of a congregation of millions, he said, "I have sinned." A. Jimmy Swaggart

Q. What late actor and political figure was the mayor of Palm Springs in 1988 and a congressman soon afterward?
A. Sonny Bono

Q. She is once again the Pakistani prime minister. A. Benazir Bhutto

Q. Lockerbie, Scotland, saw this disaster. A. Crash of Pan Am Flight 103

Q. In 1989 Jaron Lanier invented this nascient gaming technology.   A. Virtual reality

Q. She divorced Mark Phillips in 1989.   A. Princess Anne

Q. Baseball pitcher who battled cancer in his pitching arm.   A. Dave Dravecky

Q. This tricolor title was given to the AIDS research album.   A. *Red, White & Blue*

Q. Her father was the first Irish-American congressman from Boston, and her husband, Joe, was once the U.S.'s youngest bank president.   A. Rose Kennedy

Q. This Bolshoi dancer turned to movies such as *Witness* and *The Zone*.   A. Alexander Godunov

Q. Elia Kazan picked him for the role of Big Daddy in *Cat on a Hot Tin Roof* after seeing him punch out a heckler in a nightclub.   A. Burl Ives

Q. Joe McCarthy called him Senator Halfbright.   A. Senator Fulbright

Q. His father named him after Hall of Fame catcher Cochrane.   A. Mickey Mantle

Q. Senator John Kerry of this state married a Heinz heiress.   A. Massachusetts

Q. In 1995 it became the first new Hollywood studio in fifty-five years.   A. DreamWorks SKG

Q. The three Hollywood moguls who make up DreamWorks SKG.   A. Spielberg, Katzenberg, Geffen

Q. Two new TV networks in 1995.   A. UPN and WB

Q. Canadian liquor company and the production company it bought.   A. Seagrams bought MCA

Q. Company that bought ailing CBS.   A. Westinghouse

Q. Author of *Crossing the Threshold of Hope*.   A. Pope John Paul II

Q. Nobel Prize winner who wrote *Of Love and Other Demons*.   A. Gabriel García Marquez

Q. His book *1945* was a terrible flop, while his *To Renew America* sold great.   A. Newt Gingrich

Extreme Presidential Quiz

See how many of these questions you can answer about presidents who were first, last, oldest, youngest, or at some other extreme.

Scoring
19: Lincoln-esque
16–18: FDR-ian
12–15: Wilson-ic
8–11: Fillmore-al
<8: Nixon wannabe

1. Alphabetically, the first president.
2. Alphabetically, the last president.
3. First president born in the independent U.S., in 1784.
4. First president born in the eighteenth century, in 1804.
5. First president born in the twentieth century, in 1917.
6. First president born west of the Mississippi, in Iowa.
7. In 1856, this first Republican candidate lost to James Buchanan.
8. The first Whig president.
9. In 1852, this last Whig candidate lost to Pierce.
10. These two men have lost the most presidential campaigns—three each.
11. What future president was the first American minister to England?
12. What future president was the first civilian governor of the Philippines?
13. In 1933, FDR became the last president to be inaugurated on this day.
14. Who was the first president not from Virginia or Massachusetts?
15. Who was the youngest man elected president?
16. Who was the youngest man to serve as president?
17. What president suffered the first assassination attempt?
18. Who was the first president to die in office?
19. Who was the first, and only, bachelor president?

Answers on page 163.

Q. Creator of detective Adam Dagliesh. A. P. D. James

Q. This elder stateman of literary lawyers published short stories in 1995. A. Louis Auchincloss

Q. Born Virginia McGrath, she's an actress—oh yeah, she dances too. A. Ginger Rogers

Q. Hollywood censors in the 1940s banned the "sweater shot"—a shot of a woman in a tight sweater—because of the tight ones worn by this "Sweater Girl." A. Lana Turner

Q. Pen name of veterinarian James Alfred Wight. A. James Herriot

Q. Twins who were "Kings of Crime" in Britain. A. Kray brothers

Q. *The Chronic*, by him, was the most successful rap album ever. A. Dr. Dre

Q. She has been on the most covers of *People* magazine—at least 36 times. A. Princess Diana

Q. The husband of Lisa Hartman. A. Clint Black

FAMOUS AFRICAN-AMERICANS

As I discussed in the chapter on preparing for *Jeopardy!*, the show includes a category that expressly deals with cultural diversity at least once every week, usually more often. Also, within categories, the show includes more and more questions about African-Americans, Hispanic Americans, Asian-American history, and famous women. Here is a list of famous African-Americans that you need to know cold.

Rev. Dr. Ralph David Abernathy	Organizer, 1957, and president, 1968, of the Southern Christian Leadership Conference
Maya Angelou	Author who read her poem "On the Pulse of Morning" at Pres. Bill Clinton's inauguration

Crispus Attucks	Agitator who led group that precipitated the "Boston Massacre," March 5, 1770.
James Baldwin	Author, playwright: *The Fire Next Time, Blues for Mister Charlie, Just Above My Head*
Benjamin Banneker	Inventor, astronomer, mathematician, and gazetteer; served on commission that surveyed and laid out Washington, D.C.
Imamu Amiri Baraka	b LeRoi Jones, 1934, poet, playwright, wrote *Preface to a 20 Volume Suicide*
Dr. Mary McCleod Bethune	Adviser to presidents Franklin Roosevelt and Harry Truman; founder, president, Bethune-Cookman College
Thomas Bradley	Mayor of Los Angeles, 1973–93
Dr. Ralph Bunche	First black to win the Nobel Peace Prize, 1950; undersecretary of the UN, 1950
George Washington Carver	Botanist, chemurgist, and educator; his extensive experiments in soil building and plant diseases revolutionized the economy of the South; discovered hundreds of uses for the peanut, sweet potato, and soybean
Shirley Chisholm	First black women elected to U.S. House of Representatives, Brooklyn, NY, 1968
David Dinkins	First black mayor of New York City, 1990–93

Frederick Douglass	Author, editor, orator, diplomat who edited the abolitionist weekly, *The North Star*, in Rochester, NY; U.S. minister and consul general to Haiti; wrote *Life and Times of Frederick Douglass*
Dr. Charles Richard Drew	Pioneers in development of blood banks
William Edward Burghardt (W.E.B.) Du Bois	Historian, sociologist, and founder of the National Association for the Advancement of Colored People (NAACP)

CIVICS CLASS

If you are still in high school when you buy this book, please pay attention in your civics class. *Jeopardy!* loves to test people on our government. Do you know which amendment is the "Venus de Milo" amendment, for example? (The second; it guarantees the right to bear arms.) Answer these questions about our government and national symbols.

Q. After the vice-president, who is next in line to succeed to the presidency? A. Speaker of the House

Q. During what war did the U.S. adopt the motto "In God We Trust"? A. Civil War

Q. Who was the secretary of the treasury who first put "In God We Trust" on our coins? A. Salmon P. Chase

Q. At what fort, on July 4, 1960, was the first 50-star flag raised? A. Fort McHenry

Q. What two states, in 1912, were the last to join the Union before Alaska and Hawaii came along? A. New Mexico and Arizona

Q. What name was bestowed on our flag by Captain William Driver as he raised it on his brig, the Charles Doggett, in 1824? A. Old Glory

Q. From 1795 to 1818 the United States flag had this many stars. A. Fifteen

Q. It is the only flag that may be flown in America over the United States flag. A. The United Nations flag

Q. On this holiday the flag should be flown at half staff until noon and then be raised to its peak. A. Memorial Day

Q. What basis of an early-morning schoolroom ritual first appeared in the September 8, 1892, issue of the *Youth's Companion* magazine? A. The Pledge of Allegiance

Q. In 1957, the Library of Congress attributed authorship of the Pledge of Allegiance to this man, not James Upham, one of his editors. A. Francis Bellamy

Q. This many stripes were on the flag Francis Scott Key saw when writing "The Star-Spangled Banner." A. Fifteen

Q. This famous American was a graduate of St. John's College, Annapolis, a lawyer, and a volunteer in a light artillery company. A. Francis Scott Key

Q. This patriotic song is set to the tune "To Anacreon in Heaven." A. "The Star-Spangled Banner"

Q. Clergyman Samuel Francis Smith set his words to this patriotic song, unaware that it was the melody for "God Save the Queen." A. "America (My Country 'Tis of Thee)"

Q. This patriotic song was composed by Katherine Lee Bates after she was inspired by the view atop Pike's Peak. A. "America, the Beautiful"

Q. This American symbol bears an inscription from Leviticus: "Proclaim liberty throughout all the land unto all the inhabitants thereof." A. Liberty Bell

Q. This Frenchman designed the Statue of Liberty. A. Frederic Bartholdi

Q. Before 1956, when Eisenhower renamed it Liberty Island, this island held the Statue of Liberty. A. Bedloe's Island

Q. This president dedicated the Statue of Liberty in 1886.
A. Grover Cleveland

Q. This island, proclaimed a museum by Lyndon Johnson, was the gateway to America for 12 million immigrants.
A. Ellis Island

Q. This city hosted the First Continental Congress.   A. Philadelphia

Q. Often called the first president, this Maryland native was the first president of the Continental Congress under the Articles of Confederation.   A. John Hanson

Q. Jefferson, Adams, Franklin, Sherman, and Livingston were on the committee to draft this document.   A. The Declaration of Independence

Q. This state was the ninth, and dispositive, state to ratify the Constitution.   A. New Hampshire

Q. It was the thirteenth state.   A. Rhode Island

Q. This was the first state, after the original thirteen, to ratify the Constitution.   A. Vermont

Q. The first American Constitution to abolish the African slave trade.   A. The Confederate Constitution

Q. Father Junipero Serra founded what city?   A. San Diego

Q. Under the 25th Amendment, this secretary is the first cabinet member in line for the presidency.   A. Secretary of State

Q. The Customs Service and the Bureau of Alcohol, Tobacco, and Firearms are division of this cabinet department.
A. Treasury

Q. This cabinet department was eliminated in 1970.   A. Post Office

Q. Food stamps and the Forestry Service are governed by this cabinet department.   A. Agriculture

Q. The census is administered by this cabinet department.
A. Commerce

Q. This third chief justice served longer than any other.
A. John Marshall

Q. He was the first Jewish justice on the Supreme Court.
A. Louis Brandeis

Q. He served in the Supreme Court from 1939 to 1975, longer than anyone else. A. William O. Douglas

Q. He was the last president not to appoint any Supreme Court justices. A. Jimmy Carter

Q. This article of the Constitution specifies the method of its amendation. A. Article Five

Q. This article sets out the ratification process for the Constitution. A. Article Seven

---

Answers to Quizzes

Answers to Extreme Presidential Quiz

1. John Adams
2. Woodrow Wilson
3. Martin Van Buren
4. Franklin Pierce
5. Jimmy Carter
6. Herbert Hoover
7. John C. Frémont
8. William Henry Harrison
9. Winfield Scott
10. Henry Clay
    William Jennings Bryan
11. John Adams
12. William Howard Taft
13. March 4
14. Andrew Jackson
15. John F. Kennedy
16. Theodore Roosevelt
17. Andrew Jackson
18. William Henry Harrison
19. James Buchanan

CHAPTER 11

North American Geography

If I had to pick the single subject that comes up most often on *Jeopardy!* it would have to be geography. One reason is that it is such a huge field of knowledge. Another reason is that so many other categories, like "Travel," "Cooking," or "Museums" ultimately end up being about geography. So here are some tough quizzes. To be a champion, you should be able to get 70 percent of these questions right.

SOME LISTS TO MEMORIZE

State capitals
State nicknames
Major city airports
Major land acquisitions
Rivers that form the borders of states

SOURCES OF QUICK INFORMATION

AAA Tour Guides for various states
The Dictionary of Cultural Literacy, pp. 375–89 (American geography)

New York Public Library Desk Reference, 2d ed., pp. 790–92 (state symbols)

BODIES OF WATER

Did you know that Niagara Falls moves backwards every year? Yup, erosion causes it to recede two inches each year. Rivers, bays, waterfalls, and lakes are popular *Jeopardy!* topics. Take this tough quiz to see how many you know.

Q. What river rises in the Southern Rockies, flows through west Texas, and empties in the Rio Grande? A. Pecos

Q. The headwaters of the Missouri are in this state. A. Montana

Q. This river flows from southern West Virginia to Pittsburgh, joining the Allegheny to make the Ohio. A. Monongahela

Q. This river is navigable from East Brady, Pennsylvania, to Pittsburgh. A. Allegheny

Q. This Arizona river that flows into the Colorado shares its name with a poisonous lizard. A. Gila

Q. What river flows into the Columbia at the Oregon/Washington border? A. Snake

Q. River that flows into the Sacramento River in the Central Valley. A. San Joaquin

Q. Though Nebraska is most associated with this river, the south branch of it flows through Denver. A. Platte

Q. The Chatahoochee River forms part of Georgia's border with this state. A. Alabama

Q. River that forms Nebraska's border with Iowa and South Dakota. A. Missouri

Q. The two great lakes connected by Lake St. Clair. A. Huron and Erie

Q. Saginaw Bay is part of this great lake. A. Lake Huron

Q. Ponca, Nebraska, is the northernmost navigable point on this mighty river. A. Missouri

Q. The Ouachita River, a tributary of the Mississippi, nearly bisects this state. A. Arkansas

Q. This "colorful" river rises near Amarillo, Texas, and flows through Shreveport, Louisiana, before joining the Mississippi. *A.* Red River

Q. Mexico calls this river Rio Bravo del Norte. *A.* Rio Grande

Q. This river flows out of Lake Winnipeg and forms the North Dakota/Minnesota border. *A.* Red River of the North

Q. The Milk and Yellowstone rivers flow into this great river, which shares its name with a state. *A.* Missouri

Q. The Trinity, Brazos, Nueces, and Sabine rivers touch or are in this state. *A.* Texas

Q. Three rivers flowing through New York City. *A.* East, Harlem, and Hudson

TOUGH QUESTIONS ABOUT MOUNTAINS, PLATEAUS, AND DESERTS

Q. The Wasatch Range of mountains is mostly in what state? *A.* Utah

Q. The Ozark plateau is not in Arkansas but in this northern neighbor. *A.* Missouri

Q. The Boston Mountains are not in Massachusetts but are mostly in this state. *A.* Arkansas

Q. Part of the Appalachian Mountains that runs through West Virginia, Pennsylvania, and southern New York state. *A.* Allegheny

Q. Mountains of northern New England. *A.* White

Q. Mountains of northern New York. *A.* Adirondacks

Q. Range that separates Idaho and Montana. *A.* Bitterroot

Q. Range that Mt. Whitney is in. *A.* Sierra Nevada

Q. Desert in southern Arizona and Mexico. *A.* Sonoran Desert

Q. Range that traverses northern Alaska. *A.* Brooks Range

Q. The highest point in Washington State. *A.* Mt. Rainier

Q. The Bighorn Mountains are in these two states. *A.* Montana and Wyoming

Q. The Harney Basin makes up the western portion of what state? A. Oregon

A GEOGRAPHY CATEGORY THAT YOU MUST KNOW:
STATE NICKNAMES

There are many state symbols, such as flowers, trees, songs, mottoes, and more. You only need to know the state nicknames. *Jeopardy!* will not expect you to know the state bird of Rhode Island, for example (the Rhode Island Red).

Q. This state has the little-known nickname of the Camellia State. A. Alabama

Q. Though it may not apply to Jim Guy Tucker at the moment, this state is the Land of Opportunity. A. Arkansas

Q. Besides Peach State, the other nickname of Georgia. A. Empire State of the South

Q. This is the Gem State. A. Idaho

Q. The Prairie State; Lincoln lived here during his "prairie years." A. Illinois

Q. Nickname of Kansas. A. Sunflower State

Q. The Old Line or Free State. A. Maryland

Q. Flowering tree that provides the nickname of Mississippi. A. Magnolia

Q. Montana is not the mountain state, this one is. A. West Virginia

Q. Nickname for Montana. A. Treasure State

Q. Because it was admitted during the Civil War, this state was called the Battle Born State. A. Nevada

Q. The largest city in the Granite State. A. Manchester

Q. During the Civil War, soldiers from North Carolina were said to hold their positions as if they had these. A. Tarheels

Q. Magical nickname of New Mexico. A. Land of Enchantment

Q. New Jersey is the Garden State. What state is the Peace Garden State? A. North Dakota

Q. Connecticut merchants are alleged to have sold sawdust as this, hence Connecticut's nickname.   A. Nutmeg

STATE NAME WORDPLAY

Try these quizzes about the letters and words that make up the names of states.

Q. While North and South Carolina have as many letters in their names, this state has the longest one-word name. A. Massachusetts

Q. The three shortest names.   A. Utah, Iowa, and Ohio

Q. The only state name ending in three vowels.   A. Hawaii

Q. The only state name ending in three consonants.   A. Massachusetts

Q. It is the only state with one neighbor and one syllable in its name.   A. Maine

Q. Of the states named for people, the only two that were not in the original thirteen.   A. Washington and Louisiana

Q. George for whom Georgia is named.   A. George II

Q. Maryland was named for this queen of Charles I of England.   A. Henrietta Maria

Q. This English king has two states named for him and one for his wife.   A. Charles I

Q. The Duke of York, for whom New York is named, later became this king.   A. James II

Q. Louis for whom Louisiana is named.   A. Louis XIV

STATE CAPITAL QUESTIONS

I cannot even count the number of times that the Final Jeopardy! clue has been about state capitals. This category can be very important. Try out these questions, any of which could be a Final Jeopardy! question.

Q. Four state capitals named for presidents.   A. Madison, Jackson, Jefferson City, and Lincoln

Q. The only three-word state capital. A. Salt Lake City
Q. This state capital has the largest population. A. Phoenix
Q. This state capital has the smallest population.
  A. Montpelier
Q. Founded in 1610, it is the oldest U.S. state capital.
  A. Santa Fe
Q. Northernmost state capital in the forty-eight contiguous
  states. A. Bismarck
Q. Southernmost state capital. A. Honolulu
Q. Southernmost state capital in the forty-eight contiguous
  states. A. Austin
Q. Easternmost state capital. A. Augusta
Q. Westernmost state capital in the forty-eight contiguous
  states. A. Salem
Q. The Duke of York who became James II was also the Duke
  of this, the name of a state capital. A. Albany
Q. This state capital, the site of the U.S. Naval Academy, was
  named for the Queen of England in 1702. A. Annapolis
  (for Queen Anne)
Q. State capital named for a western hero. A. Carson City
Q. The three state capitals located on the Missouri River.
  A. Jefferson City, Pierre, and Bismarck
Q. The River Jordan flows through this state capital founded
  by religious settlers. A. ˙Salt Lake City
Q. State capital located on the South Platte River. A. Denver
Q. The only state capital located on the Colorado River, it's
  not Denver or Phoenix. A. Austin

CHAPTER 12

World Geography

This is such a huge category that it warrants a hundred questions. Any of these could be the question that gets you that Daily Double. Study hard; these will come up.

SOME LISTS TO MEMORIZE

World capitals
Superlatives: Longest rivers, largest countries, highest mountains—in the world and by continent
Places that have changed their names

SOURCES OF QUICK INFORMATION

Dictionary of Cultural Literacy, pp. 332–74
"Nations of the World," *World Almanac*

100 MOST IMPORTANT FACTS IN WORLD GEOGRAPHY

This category will take you far on *Jeopardy!* The best way to learn it is to study the map and memorize your lists. You might also look at some travel books about various European countries, because the writers love to ask travel questions. But to start, learn these hundred most important facts about world geography.

Q. What city on Mexico's Pacific coast is known for its beaches and cliff divers? A. Acapulco

Q. What arm of the Mediterranean Sea juts up between Italy and Yugoslavia? A. Adriatic Sea

Q. Literally "White Mountain" in French, what is the highest peak in France? A. Mont Blanc

Q. What name is given to the periodic winds that both ravage and nourish India? A. Monsoons

Q. What largest city of Monaco is famous for its gambling casinos? A. Monte Carlo

Q. Literally meaning "mountain view," what is the capital of Uruguay? A. Montevideo

Q. Located in North America, what is the second largest French-speaking city in the world? A. Montreal

Q. In what city would you find Gorki Central Park?
A. Moscow

Q. In A.D. 79, Herculaneum, Stabiae, and Pompeii were buried by what volcano? A. Mt. Vesuvius

Q. In what southeast African country with its capital at Maputo does the Zambezi River meet the sea? A. Mozambique

Q. What commercial and industrial center is the capital of the German state of Bavaria? A. Munich

Q. What city, formerly the capital of British East Africa, became the capital of Kenya upon the country's independence? A. Nairobi

Q. What two countries combined to form Tanzania? A. Tanganyika and Zanzibar

Q. According to its name, what major southwest Italian seaport is the "new city"? A. Naples (short for Neopolis)

Q. What two kingdoms in central Asia are bordered by China to the north and by India to the west, south, and east?
A. Nepal and Bhutan

Q. What lowland country's name literally means "lowlands"?
A. Netherlands

Q. In 1929, what city replaced Calcutta as the capital of India? A. New Delhi

Q. Although Wellington is the capital of New Zealand, what is the country's largest city? A. Auckland

Q. As the name implies, what province became Canada's tenth and "newest," province in 1949? A. Newfoundland

Q. What republic in Central America is bordered by Honduras to the north and Costa Rica to the south?
A. Nicaragua

Q. What city with a "pleasant" name is the most famous French resort on the Riviera? A. Nice

Q. What West African nation suffered through the ill-fated Biafra independence movement in 1967? A. Nigeria

Q. Although the Nile is the longest river in the world, which river carries the most water every day? A. Amazon (the second longest)

Q. What sea separates Norway from northern England?
A. North Sea

Q. What did French settlers, expelled from the area in the 1750s, call Nova Scotia? A. Acadia

Q. The term "Orient" applies to the Far East. What is the equivalent term applied to the West? A. Occident

Q. What is the Canadian province with the largest population? A. Ontario

Q. What is the present name of the region once called East Pakistan? A. Bangladesh

Q. In 1903, backed by the U.S., Panama revolted against what southern neighbor, of which it was a part then?
A. Colombia

Q. The fabled stone fortress of Macchu Picchu was the remains of what ancient empire? A. Incan

Q. The Vistula River, which flows into the Baltic Sea, flows through what European capital? A. Warsaw

Q. With its capital at Charlottetown, what is Canada's smallest province? A. Prince Edward Island

Q. In the nineteenth century, which German state led the unification movement in that country? A. Prussia

Q. Although it is Korea's oldest city, most traces of this North Korean capital's three-thousand-year history were destroyed under Japanese occupation and in the Korean War? A. Pyongyang

Q. Extending from the Bay of Biscay to the Mediterranean, what mountain chain separates France from Spain? A. Pyrenees

Q. What river rises in the Alps, then flows generally north through or bordering Switzerland, Liechtenstein, Germany, France, and Holland before reaching the North Sea? A. Rhine

Q. What nation was formerly called Rhodesia? A. Zimbabwe

Q. What Brazilian city received its name because it was discovered in the month of January? A. Rio de Janiero

Q. What is an alternate name for the beautiful French coast sometimes called the Côte d'Azur? A. Riviera

Q. What second largest Dutch city is one of the largest ports in the world? A. Rotterdam

Q. The famous Paris-to-Dakar off-road vehicle race ends in what country? A. Senegal

Q. What Brazilian city is the largest city in South America? A. São Paulo

Q. What vast farming province lies north of North Dakota and Montana and has its capital at Regina? A. Saskatchewan

Q. What name is given to the tropical grasslands with scattered trees prevalent in Africa? A. Savanna

Q. Though Edinburgh is the capital of Scotland, what is its largest city? A. Glasgow

Q. What Chinese port city is the most populous city in the most populous country in the world? A. Shanghai

Q. What triangle-shaped island is the largest in the Mediterranean? A. Sicily

Q. What West African country, whose name means "mountains of the lion," was a destination for some freed slaves and has its capital at Freetown? A. Sierra Leone

Q. What peninsula is formed by the Mediterranean Sea, the Gulf of Suez, and the Gulf of Aqaba? A. Sinai Peninsula

---

Quick Quiz Surprise! You Speak Malaysian

Believe it or not, you and I speak lots of different languages every day when we use foreign words that have entered our language. Here are some that the *Jeopardy!* writers might like; see if you can get them.

1. What red, powdery spice is literally just "pepper" in Hungarian?
2. Malaysian word for "tasty," it's a ubiquitous condiment.
3. Japanese for the star cluster "the Pleiades," it's a Japanese car company whose symbol is seven stars.
4. Speaking of Japanese cars, what company's name means "three diamonds" in Japanese?
5. What Japanese ice skater is a little "green" behind the ears, according to her first name?
6. Malaysian for "man of the forest," it is now indigenouos to only Borneo and Sumatra.
7. Don't wait to answer this English word, which means "hold for tomorrow" in Latin.
8. What tan color takes its name from the Hindi word for "dusty"?
9. Indonesian word for "dyed," it's a method of dying fabric using dye-resistant wax.
10. What type of entertainer, such as Edgar Bergen, is literally a "stomach talker" in French?

Answers on page 180.

Q. Located at the tip of the Malay Peninsula, what city is one of the world's busiest ports?   A. Singapore

Q. Formerly Northern Rhodesia, what African country has Lusaka as its capital?   A. Zambia

Q. Its capital, Harare, used to be called Salisbury, and the country itself used to be called Rhodesia. What is its present name?   A. Zimbabwe

Q. What Arabian peninsula nations recently merged under Communist leadership?   A. Yemen

Q. On what teardrop-shaped island are Tamil and Sinhalese rebels currently fighting for power?   A. Sri Lanka

Q. Each year, all of the Nobel Prizes except the Peace Prize are awarded in what city?   A. Stockholm

Q. What country bordered by Egypt, Ethiopia, the Red Sea, Kenya, and Uganda is the biggest by area in Africa?
A. Sudan

Q. What large, cigar-shaped island, though covered in impenetrable forest, provides half of Indonesia's income, producing oil, gold, silver, and rubber?   A. Sumatra

Q. The intellectual and business center of German-speaking Switzerland, this city is also the country's largest.
A. Zurich

Q. What small kingdom, bordered by Mozambique on one side and South Africa on all other sides, has a name that sounds something like a landlocked European nation's?
A. Swaziland

Q. Although Bern is the capital of Switzerland, what is its largest city?   A. Zurich

Q. What city, the first settlement of British convicts in Australia, is now the largest in that country?   A. Sydney

Q. Home to both Robert Louis Stevenson and Paul Gauguin for a while, what is the largest island in French Polynesia?   A. Tahiti

Q. What do we now call the country once called Siam?
A. Thailand

Q. What region in southwestern China was once ruled by the Dalai Lama?   A. Tibet

Q. What city in Mexico's Baja California state is just across the border from San Diego?   A. Tijuana

Q. Now a village in central Mali, what famed West African city was a major trade center in the fourteenth century?
A. Timbuktu

Q. What independent republic in the Caribbean Sea consists of two islands off the coast of Venezuela and has its capital at Port-of-Spain?   A. Trinidad and Tobago

Q. The sun is directly over this imaginary line, located at 23^{1}/$_3$ degrees north latitude at the summer solstice?   A. Tropic of Cancer

Q. The city of Carthage, enemy of Rome in the Punic Wars, was located in what is now this African country.
A. Tunisia

Q. The Ottoman Empire emerged in Anatolia, which is the larger portion of what modern country?   A. Turkey

Q. Uganda is landlocked with regard to oceans, but does reside on what lake?   A. Lake Victoria

Q. Which of the new countries formed by the disintegration of the U.S.S.R. is often called the breadbasket of Russia?
A. The Ukraine

Q. Extending from the Arctic tundra to the desert north of the Caspian Sea, what mountains separate Europe and Asia?   A. Urals

Q. Named for a British explorer, what British Columbian city is a major tourist center and moviemaking center on the Pacific Coast?   A. Vancouver

Q. From what European city does the country of Venezuela get its name?   A. Venice

Q. What city was the capital of the Austro-Hungarian Empire and home to the Hapsburg dynasty?   A. Vienna

Q. What principal waterway of western Russia is the longest river in Europe?   A. Volga

Q. What wall, containing stones from the original Temple of Solomon in Jerusalem, is a Jewish holy place commemorating their sorrows from earliest times?   A. Wailing Wall

Q. Cambria was the Roman name for what part of Great Britain, which has its capital at Cardiff?   A. Wales

Q. All English monarchs since William the Conqueror have been crowned in the same church, located in London. What is it?   A. Westminster Abbey

---

Geographic Name Origins

Jeopardy! loves word origin questions and geography. Here's a combination. Name the place name which means or is derived from each of the following.

1. Huge icy island to which Eric the Red gave a misleading name to attract settlers.

2. Small african country whose name means "Mountains of the Lion" and whose capital is Freetown

3. U.S. state discovered by Spaniards on the Feast of Flowers

4. South African province discovered on Christmas Day, hence its name referring to "birth"

5. Famed Ecuadoran islands named after the large tortoises there

6. "Dry" Caribbean islands whose name means "turtles" in Spanish

7. Island prison whose name is literally "the Pelican" in Spanish

8. Pacific Island group whose name reflects the belief that a wise king used gold from them in building the Temple in Jerusalem

Answers on page 180.

Q. Rising in Tibet, flowing through central China, and meeting the Pacific Ocean at Shanghai, what is the longest river in Asia? A. Yangtze

Q. Many ancient Mayan ruins, including the famous Chichen Itza, are located in what Mexican peninsula, which juts out into the Caribbean Sea? A. Yucatán

Q. What Canadian territory is bordered by Alaska to the west, the Arctic Ocean to the north, and the Northwest Territories to the east? A. The Yukon

Q. What present nation was once Zaire and, before that, the Belgian Congo? A. Democratic Republic of the Congo

Q. An arm of the Mediterranean Sea between Greece and Turkey, it was named for the father of Theseus, who, believing his son dead, hurled himself into it. A. Aegean Sea

Q. What south-central Asian republic was invaded by Soviet troops in 1979? A. Afghanistan

Q. Banff National Park, a popular vacation spot, is located in the Canadian Rockies in what province, which has Edmonton as its capital? A. Alberta

Q. What port city, named for a Macedonian conqueror, is located in the delta of the Nile River? A. Alexandria

Q. This capital city has the most canals of any European city, beating even Venice. What is this capital of the Netherlands? A. Amsterdam

Q. Running from Colombia to the Tierra del Fuego, what are the primary mountains of South America? A. Andes

Q. Since achieving independence from Portugal, what southwest African nation has endured years of civil war, exacerbated by Cuban interference? A. Angola

Q. The Aleutians, the Hawaiian Islands, or the Azores: All of these are groups of islands in a chain, related by the geologic event that created them. What do we call such a group of islands? A. Archipelago

Q. After Brazil, what nation is second largest in area in South America? A. Argentina

Famous Structures Around the World

The only man-made object visible from space	Great Wall of China
Most famous structure in Agra, India	Taj Mahal
Rediscovered ancient religious center in Cambodia	Angkor Wat
Only Wonder of the Ancient World still standing	Great Pyramids
Only Wonder of the Ancient World that was alive	Hanging Gardens of Babylon
City that has the Spanish Steps	Rome, Italy
The statue of the Little Mermaid guards this city's harbor	Copenhagen, Denmark
The Grand Coulee Dam crosses what mighty Northwest river?	Columbia
Palace where you'll find the "Hall of Mirrors"	Versailles
Pacific island where Europeans discovered huge black statues	Easter Island
Central part of Peking where the emperor lived	Forbidden City
Great Moorish castle in Granada, Spain	Alhambra
Home of British kings and queens	Buckingham Palace
Australian city whose opera house looks like stacked eggshells	Sydney
City with CN Tower	Toronto, Canada

Q. In 1956, the Russians took over after the United States and Britain withdrew funding for what large Egyptian dam across the Nile? A. The Aswan High Dam

Q. What is the name of the hill in Athens that houses the Erectheum and the Parthenon? A. Acropolis

Q. What is the name for a small island consisting of a coral reef that surrounds a lagoon? A. Atoll

Q. In what country can you find the islands of Bali, Celebes, part of Borneo, Java, and Sumatra? A. Indonesia

Q. What peninsula contains the countries of Romania, Bulgaria, Greece, Albania, and part of Turkey? A. Balkan Peninsula

Q. What arm of the Indian Ocean is located between India, Sri Lanka, and Burma? A. Bay of Bengal

Q. If you wanted to go from the U.S. to Russia and travel the shortest distance, you'd go across what strait between Alaska and Siberia? A. Bering Strait

---

Answers to Quizzes

Answers to Surprise! You Speak Malaysian Quiz

1. Paprika	6. Orangutan
2. Ketchup	7. Procrastinate
3. Subaru	8. Khaki
4. Mitsubishi	9. Batik or batique
5. Midori Ito	10. Ventriloquist

Answers to Geographic Name Origins Quiz

1. Greenland	5. Galápagos
2. Sierra Leone	6. Tortugas
3. Florida	7. Alcatraz
4. Natal	8. Solomon Islands

CHAPTER 13

Literature

An Incomplete Education, pp. 4–44 (American literature), 182–261 (literature). Start with this book. It is the best and easiest way to become immediately well versed in the basics of literature that *Jeopardy!* asks about. Plus, it is loads of fun to read.

World Almanac and Book of Facts, "Noted Writers of the Past" under "Writers" in the "Quick Reference Index" at the end of the book. This list should be memorized by rote.

All of the entries in *The Bathroom Book, vols. 1–4*

Benét's Reader's Encyclopedia

New York Public Library Desk Reference, 2d ed., pp. 183–89 (playwrights), 206–29 (literature)

The Dictionary of Cultural Literacy, pp. 81–139 (world literature)

THE 100 MOST IMPORTANT FACTS ABOUT LITERATURE

Although geography is my best subject, literature categories were where I usually had the greatest advantage over my opponents. It seems that few people really know literature anymore. Because of this, you can gain an advantage, too, if you know even a little bit about literature. Here are a hundred facts you simply need to know.

Q. What novel by Emily Brontë concerned the thwarted love of two young people, Catherine and Heathcliff, and the cruelty Heathcliff inflicts as a result?   A. *Wuthering Heights*

Q. What leading poet of the Romantic movement in literature gave us the image of "a host of golden daffodils" waving in the breeze?   A. William Wordsworth

Q. L. Frank Baum got the title for what book from the label on the second drawer of his filing cabinet (the first was labeled *A-N*)?   A. *The Wonderful Wizard of Oz*

Q. By what name do we better know the American playwright who was born Thomas Lanier Williams and who wrote *Cat on a Hot Tin Roof*?   A. Tennessee Williams

Q. What are the first two names of the son of writer A. A. Milne?   A. Christopher Robin

Q. What Irish-born author of *The Importance of Being Earnest* wrote *The Ballad of Reading Gaol* while in prison for homosexuality?   A. Oscar Wilde

Q. When the students in *Dead Poets' Society* stood on their desks and said "O Captain! My Captain," they were quoting what American poet?   A. Walt Whitman

Q. Though he wrote a well-received history of the world, what British writer is most famous for writing *War of the Worlds*?   A. H. G. Wells

Q. Finish this famous line from "The Rime of the Ancient Mariner" by Coleridge: Water, water, everywhere...
   A. Nor any drop to drink

Q. In what book, named for the pond near which he wrote it, does Thoreau state, "The mass of men lead lives of quiet desperation"?   A. *Walden*

Q. What period of literature is named for the monarch of England who reigned from 1837 to 1901?   A. Victorian

Q. What novel by William Makepeace Thackeray features Becky Sharp, an unscrupulous woman who gains wealth through cleverness?   A. *Vanity Fair*

Q. What Harriet Beecher Stowe title character was a pious, passive slave who was eventually beaten to death by Simon Legree, his overseer?   A. Uncle Tom

Q. What did poet Joyce Kilmer think that he would never see a poem as lovely as?   A. A tree

Q. In what novel does a young boy, Jim Hawkins, join with two men in hiring a ship to look for treasure?   A. *Treasure Island*

Q. According to William Blake, what animal was "burning bright, in the forests of the night"?   A. Tiger

Q. In *A Christmas Carol* by Dickens, who says the famous line, "God bless us, every one"?   A. Tiny Tim Cratchit

Q. What author and cartoonist told us about *The Secret Life of Walter Mitty* and put us in *The Catbird Seat*?   A. James Thurber

Q. In which Lewis Carroll work does Alice meet Tweedledum and Tweedledee?   A. *Through the Looking-Glass*

Q. Gandhi and Martin Luther King Jr. both based their philosophies in part on what American author's essay "Civil Disobedience"?   A. Henry David Thoreau

Q. What English poet, who went blind late in life, wrote "they also serve who only stand and wait" in his poem "On His Blindness"?   A. John Milton

Q. What Shakespearean king, when thinking about the treachery of his eldest two daughters, said, "That way madness lies," and decided not to dwell on them?   A. King Lear

Q. What poet laureate of England wrote about the disastrous "Charge of the Light Brigade?"   A. Alfred, Lord Tennyson

Q. What Ernest Hemingway novel deals with a group of young Americans living in Europe in the 1920s—the so-called Lost Generation?   A. *The Sun Also Rises*

Q. What Tennessee Williams play tells of the decline and tragic end of Blanche DuBois, a southern belle who has "always depended upon the kindness of strangers"?   A. *A Streetcar Named Desire*

Q. During the Civil War, Abraham Lincoln is reputed to have said to what author, "So you are the little woman who started this big war"?   A. Harriet Beecher Stowe

Q. What leader of the women's liberation movement was the founder of *Ms.* magazine?   A. Gloria Steinem

Q. What John Steinbeck work tells of the Joad family's journey across the U.S. in search of work?   A. *The Grapes of Wrath*

Q. What author of *The Autobiography of Alice B. Toklas* coined the term "the Lost Generation"?   A. Gertrude Stein

Q. What Shakespearean character states, "Something is rotten in the state of Denmark"?   A. Marcellus in *Hamlet*

Q. According to a Whittier poem, who said to Confederate troops, "Shoot if you must this old gray head, but spare your country's flag"?   A. Barbara Frietchie

Q. To what type of bird was Percy Bysshe Shelley speaking when he said, "Hail to thee, blithe Spirit!"?   A. Skylark

Q. What Irish playwright penned *Pygmalion*, upon which the musical *My Fair Lady* was loosely based?   A. George Bernard Shaw

Q. What name did James Hilton, author of *Lost Horizon*, give to his fictional land of peace and perpetual youth?   A. Shangri-La

Q. In the Shakespearean sonnet, what "seasonal" question precedes "Thou art more lovely and more temperate?"   A. Shall I compare thee to a summer's day?

Q. Theo LeSieg, a children's author, is actually Theodore Geisel (Lesieg in reverse). How do we better know him?   A. Dr. Seuss

Q. In a Charles Dickens story, who was the former business partner of Jacob Marley?   A. Ebenezer Scrooge

Q. Robin Hood made an early appearance in what Scottish author's *Ivanhoe*? *A.* Sir Walter Scott

Q. What did the *A* stand for on Hester Prynne's dress? *A.* Adultery

Q. What American author was famous for his poems about Chicago and his biography of Abraham Lincoln? *A.* Carl Sandburg

Q. What African-American author penned the multigenerational *Roots*? *A.* Alex Haley

Q. Alexander Selkirk, who was stranded on a deserted island in the 1600s, was the model for what Defoe character? *A.* Robinson Crusoe

Q. What author chose the Catskill Mountains in his home state of New York as the site where Rip Van Winkle fell asleep for twenty years? *A.* Washington Irving

Q. What late nineteenth-century novel about a young man whose romantic notions of heroism in combat are smashed by the Civil War was written by Stephen Crane? *A.* *The Red Badge of Courage*

Q. According to the title of an Edgar Allan Poe poem, who was "gently rapping, rapping" at the narrator's chamber door? *A.* The raven

Q. What Jane Austen novel depicts the complex events leading up to the marriages of the two eldest daughters of the Bennet family? *A.* *Pride and Prejudice*

Q. In *The Merchant of Venice*, what did the cruel moneylender demand as a result of the merchant's breach of contract? *A.* A pound of flesh

Q. What collection of periodicals by Ben Franklin contained the line "Early to bed and early to rise, makes a man healthy, wealthy and wise"? *A.* *Poor Richard's Almanack*

Q. In the Eleanor H. Porter book, who was the ever-optimistic orphan girl who remained cheerful even in the face of adversity? *A.* *Pollyanna*

Q. In a poem by Robert Browning, who freed the city of Hamelin, Germany, of rats? *A.* The Pied Piper

Q. What American wit, and member of the Algonquin Round Table, is famous for saying, "Men seldom make passes at girls who wear glasses"?   A. Dorothy Parker

Q. In what epic poem about the rebellion and fall of Satan does John Milton state his aim as to "justify the ways of God to men"?   A. "Paradise Lost"

Q. According to the Edward Lear poem, who "went to sea in a pea green boat?"   A. The Owl and the Pussycat

Q. What man, born Eric Blair, brought us the depictions of totalitarianism in *Animal Farm* and *1984*?   A. George Orwell

Q. What American playwright won four Pulitzer Prizes, for plays such as *Long Day's Journey Into Night* and *Strange Interlude*?   A. Eugene O'Neill

Q. The line "Beauty is truth, truth beauty—that is all / Ye know on earth, and all ye need to know," comes from whose poem, entitled "Ode on a Grecian Urn"?   A. John Keats

Q. According to Mark Antony, which of Caesar's assassins did he consider "the noblest Roman of them all" in Shakespeare's *Julius Caesar*?   A. Brutus

Q. In what novel do we find Winston Smith living in the nation of Oceania and battling doublespeak and the thought police?   A. *1984*

Q. What novel opens with the famous line "Call me Ishmael"?   A. *Moby Dick*

Q. What was Louisa May Alcott's sequel to *Little Women*?   A. *Little Men*

Q. What author criticized evangelism in his novel *Elmer Gantry*?   A. Sinclair Lewis

Q. What author's *Lady Chatterley's Lover* was banned as obscene in both the U.S. and Britain?   A. D. H. Lawrence

Q. "How the Elephant Got Its Trunk" is one of what author's *Just So Stories*?   A. Rudyard Kipling

Q. In a series of novels about the English upper classes, what name did P. G. Wodehouse give to Bertie Wooster's butler? A. Jeeves

Q. What title heroine served as the governess to the ward of the mysterious and moody Edward Rochester, who, though married to an insane woman, proposed to said heroine? A. *Jane Eyre*

Q. What author's *Portrait of a Lady* was recently made into a hit film? A. Henry James

Q. In what novel do factory workers stay drugged on Soma and do people reproduce by a cloning method? A. *Brave New World*

Q. What African-American author and leader of the Harlem Renaissance wondered, "What happens to a dream deferred? / Does it dry up like a raisin in the sun?" A. Langston Hughes

Q. In *Huckleberry Finn*, what was the name of the runaway slave befriended by Huck who goes with him down the river? A. Jim

Q. The lady in *Portrait of a Lady*. A. Isabel Archer

Q. Austen hero who is rich, smart, and comfortable but has the bad habit of trying to run other people's lives. A. Emma Woodhouse

Q. Hero, of sorts, of *Portrait of the Artist as a Young Man* and *Ulysses*. A. Stephen Dedalus

Q. Seeing Clym Yeobright as her ticket to glamour and freedom from the heath, she eventually realizes he's not and drowns in a bog in *Return of the Native*. A. Eustacia Vye

Q. Narrator of *Lord Jim* and *Heart of Darkness*. A. Marlow

Q. Virginia Woolf's concept of feminine perfection, Mrs. Ramsay, is from this novel. A. *To the Lighthouse*

Q. Eliot's play *Murder in the Cathedral* deals with Thomas à Becket's conflicts with this king over the latter's desire to limit the privileges of the clergy. A. Henry II

Q. In one of her plays, she condemns the new breed of south-
erners as rapacious and ruthless, like "the little foxes who
spoil the vine" of biblical verse.   A. Lillian Hellman

Q. Though published seven years after *The Little Foxes* this
Lillian Hellman play deals with an earlier stage in the lives
of the Hubbard family.   A. *Another Part of the Forest*

Q. One of the first successful anti-Nazi plays on the American
stage, this Lillian Hellman work concerns a German ref-
ugee who kills an informer who recognized him.   A. *Watch
on the Rhine*

Q. The screenplay for this 1961 film by Arthur Miller began
as a short story published in *Esquire*.   A. *The Misfits*

Q. This autobiographical play by Arthur Miller was the first
production of the Lincoln Center Repertory Theater in
New York City.   A. *After the Fall*

Q. Published in 1984, his book *Salesman in Beijing* was an account of his experiences directing one of his plays in
China.   A. Arthur Miller

Q. This American playwright is often called the playwright of
the Midwest.   A. William Inge

Q. This Clifford Odets play describes the life of a boy who
should have been a violinist but chooses an easier path to
fame, boxing.   A. *Golden Boy*

Q. His first two plays, *Waiting for Lefty* and *Awake and Sing*, established his reputation as a proletarian dramatist.
A. Clifford Odets

Q. In this trilogy of Eugene O'Neill plays, the puritan con-
science functions as the American equivalent of the Furies
in Greek myth.   A. *Mourning Becomes Electra*

Q. Ezra Mannon, a general returning from the Civil War in
Eugene O'Neill's *Mourning Becomes Electra*, is said to represent this figure from Greek myth.   A. Agamemnon

Q. The title character of this Eugene O'Neill play is the
daughter of Chris Christopherson, who sent her to be
raised in Minnesota.   A. *Anna Christie*

Q. Ephraim Cabot's new wife seduces his youngest son, gets pregnant, and then smothers the child to prove her love to the son in this O'Neill play. A. *Desire Under the Elms*

Q. The title of this Eugene O'Neill play describes either Yank, a crude stoker on a ship, or the zoo animal he releases— which kills him. A. *The Hairy Ape*

Q. The title character of this Eugene O'Neill play is a former Pullman car porter who sets himself up as ruler of a West Indian island. A. *The Emperor Jones*

Q. Through the conversations of a group of derelicts in the back room of the End of the Line Cafe, in this play Eugene O'Neill examines the value of illusions. A. *The Iceman Cometh*

Q. This Eugene O'Neill play was about the Tyrone family and Cathleen, a servant girl. A. *Long Day's Journey Into Night*

Q. This Eugene O'Neill play described a mercenary soul who cared so much about money that he did not notice that Kubla Khan's daughter was in love with him. A. *Marco Millions*

Q. After studying at Princeton, this author served in the Indiana House of Representatives, 1902–03. A. Booth Tarkington

Q. Booth Tarkington's three books about this typical twelve-year-old boy in a midwestern community were collected in an omnibus volume in 1931. A. Penrod

Q. The hero of this Tarkington novel is William Sylvanus Baxter, who is an adolescent in the throes of his first love affair. A. *Seventeen*

Q. What town does the title of the Thornton Wilder play *Our Town* refer to? A. Grover's Corners, New Hampshire

Q. What often-produced play features a Stage Manager who is a garrulous Yankee and who comments on the action as it progresses? A. *Our Town*

Q. The three acts of this popular play are "Daily Life," "Love and Marriage," and "Death." A. *Our Town*

Q. In Act II of this play, Emily Webb falls in love with, and marries, George Gibbs; in Act III, she dies during childbirth.   A. *Our Town*

Q. This Thornton Wilder play was the basis for *Hello, Dolly*.   A. *The Matchmaker*

Q. After a Franciscan friar witnesses the collapse of a Peruvian bridge, which killed five people, in this novel he wonders if it were accidental or God's design.   A. *The Bridge of San Luis Rey*

Q. Unconventional in nature, this play gives a panoramic picture of the Antrobus family, and their maid Sabina, from prehistoric times to the twentieth century.   A. *The Skin of Our Teeth*

Q. From the money this playwright earned on his earliest lyrical writings, he completed his college education at the University of Iowa.   A. Tennessee Williams

Q. His first important play, *Battle of Angels*, was unsuccessful; he rewrote it in 1957 as *Orpheus Descending*.   A. Tennessee Williams

Q. This 1951 Tennessee Williams play is a humorous treatment of a Sicilian-American woman.   A. *The Rose Tattoo*

Q. Tennessee Williams's *Camino Real* featured as a character this ubiquitous American GI.   A. Kilroy

Q. In this Tennessee Williams play, concerning a possessive mother and her homosexual son, the son is killed and devoured by a mob of starving children.   A. *Suddenly Last Summer*

Q. Tennessee Williams's *Clothes for a Summer Hotel* concerns this Jazz Age couple.   A. F. Scott and Zelda Fitzgerald

Q. Primarily a playwright, he wrote one novel, *The Roman Spring of Mrs. Stone*.   A. Tennessee Williams

Q. In Tennessee Williams's *Glass Menagerie*, the narrator of the introduction and conclusion is this character, who shortly after the play ends goes to sea.   A. Tom Wingfield

Q. One of this playwright's most famous characters, Laura Wingfield, is based on his own mentally troubled and eventually lobotomized sister. A. Tennessee Williams

Q. It is the last name of Stella, Blance Dubois's sister, in *A Streetcar Named Desire*. A. Kowalski

Q. In this play, Big Daddy Pollit is dying of cancer, so Gooper, his oldest son, schemes to get his property. A. *Cat on a Hot Tin Roof*

Q. In *Cat on a Hot Tin Roof*, Brick, the alcoholic ex-jock, is the husband of this character, nicknamed "the cat." A. Maggie

Q. In order to facilitate a reconciliation with her husband at the end of *Cat on a Hot Tin Roof*, this character falsely announces that she is pregnant. A. Maggie the Cat

Q. Ed Begley won a Best Supporting Actor Oscar for his role in this movie based on a Tennessee Williams play. A. *Sweet Bird of Youth*

Q. This first novel by James Baldwin, about the religious awakening of a fourteen-year-old black youth, was modeled closely on Baldwin's past as a storefront preacher. A. *Go Tell It on the Mountain*

Q. This American-born black author, who wrote *Notes of a Native Son*, actually lived in France from age twenty-four until age fifty-three. A. James Baldwin

Q. James Baldwin's 1986 book *Evidence of Things Not Seen* analyzed racism in light of the string of murders of black children in this city. A. Atlanta

Q. Known more for works concerning a certain foreign nation, this author also wrote five novels with an American setting under the pseudonym John Sedges. A. Pearl Buck

Q. This actor's association with José Quintero and the works of Eugene O'Neill began when he appeared as a self-loathing salesman, Hickey in *The Iceman Cometh*. A. Jason Robards

Q. This one-act play by Edward Albee is a park-bench encounter that turns deadly between a smug middle-class man and an aimless drifter.   A. *Zoo Story*

Q. Young, rich, intelligent, filled with integrity, she's the do-gooding hero of *Middlemarch*.   A. Dorothea Brooke

Q. When she still had the surname Make, she performed in Jean Genet's *Blacks*; she later wrote a famous autobiography.   A. Maya Angelou

Q. This man, who played a valet in Genet's *Blacks*, went on to become the first African-American to win the Pulitzer Prize for drama, for *No Place to Be Somebody*.   A. Charles Gordone

Q. This Arthur Miller play concerns Eddie, a longshoreman whose unspoken passion for his niece destroys him.
A. *A View From the Bridge*

Q. This novel by Willa Cather tells the story of Claude Wheeler, who grew up in the West and died in France during WWI.   A. *One of Ours*

Q. Alexandra Bergson's deep love of the land and passionate defense of the family farm dominate this Willa Cather novel.   A. *O Pioneers!*

Q. This novel is based on the lives of two eminent French clerics who attempt to build a cathedral in the American Southwest.   A. *Death Comes for the Archbishop*

Q. Mystery writer who created the character Philip Marlowe.
A. Raymond Chandler

Q. After this author was expelled from Yale in the early 1800s, he became a sailor and gentleman farmer.   A. James Fenimore Cooper

Q. This author's novel *The Pilot* is considered the first American novel of the sea.   A. James Fenimore Cooper

Q. The subtitle of this first book of the Leather-Stocking Tales by James Fenimore Cooper is *The Sources of the Susquehanna*.
A. *The Pioneers*

Q. La Longue Carabine is one of the many names this James Fenimore Cooper character goes by.   A. Natty Bumppo

Q. Who is the title character of the Cooper novel *the Last of the Mohicans?* A. Uncas

Q. Hawkeye, also known as Natty Bumppo, helped this man and his son Uncas frustrate the schemes of Magua, a Huron, in *Last of the Mohicans.* A. Chingachgook

Q. This novel in the Leather-Stocking Tales centers on the death of Natty Bumppo. A. *The Prairie*

Q. The inland sea referred to in the subtitle of this Cooper work is probably Lake Ontario, where Bumppo relinquishes the hand of Mabel Dunham. A. *The Pathfinder*

Q. Though it was the last of the Leather-Stocking Tales to be written, it deals with Natty Bumppo's youth. A. *The Deerslayer*

Categorical Poets

If *Jeopardy!* asks about a "Lake Poet" you should be able to limit your choices to three people: Wordsworth, Coleridge, or Southey. But there are other poetic groupings.

Robert Penn Warren, John Crowe Ransom	Fugitive Poets
Amy Lowell, William Carlos Williams	Imagism
Robert Herrick, Richard Lovelace	Cavalier
Anne Sexton	Confessional
George Herbert, John Donne	Metaphysical
Ralph Waldo Emerson, Margaret Fuller	Transcendentalism

ALL ABOUT SHAKESPEARE

Shakespeare is probably the most asked-about author on *Jeopardy!* Also, an amazing number of expressions and movie titles come directly from his plays. Did you know, for example, that Aldous Huxley's title *Brave New World* comes from a line from Shakespeare's *Tempest?*

To learn all about him, you can either read all thirty-seven of his plays, or you can answer these essential questions about "the Bard of Avon." Some of these are easier than others, but all of them could come up. Have fun.

Q. At eighteen, Shakespeare married this woman—she was twenty-six. A. Anne Hathaway

Q. Shakespeare's three kids. A. Susanna, Hamnet, and Judith

Q. In 1594, Shakespeare was a member of the Lord Chamberlain's Company, which became the King's Men under this king. A. James I

Q. In 1599, a group of actors from the Chamberlain's company, including Shakespeare, formed a syndicate to build and operate this new playhouse. A. Globe

Q. This theater, of which Shakespeare was part owner, was originally used for performances of plays by the Children of the Windsor Chapel. A. Blackfriars

Q. The prince of Morocco, a minor character in this Shakespearean play, warned, "All that glitters is not gold."
A. *The Merchant of Venice*

Q. This play was largely written to revive John Falstaff's character and to show him in love. A. *The Merry Wives of Windsor*

Q. This merry prankster noted, "Lord, what fools these mortals be!" A. Puck

Q. The first person this Shakespearean (and real life) king killed was his brother George, duke of Clarence.
A. Richard III

Q. In this Shakespearean play, a magician says, "We are such stuff as dreams are made on, and our little life is rounded with a sleep." A. *The Tempest*

Q. Duke Orsino, in this play, exhorts, "If music be the food of love, play on." A. *Twelfth Night*

Q. This is the only Shakespearean play to come in three parts. A. *Henry VI*

Q. The play derived from *Historia Danica* by Saxo Grammaticus.   A. *Hamlet*

Q. A complete edition of Shakespeare's works did not appear until this publication in 1623.   A. First Folio

Q. The two tasks that Helena had to perform in *All's Well That Ends Well*, in order to gain Count Bertram's love.   A. Get his ring and bear his child

Q. Character who says, "I am dying, Egypt, dying."   A. Marc Antony (*Antony and Cleopatra*)

Q. Character described thusly: "Age cannot wither her, nor custom stale her infinite variety."   A. Cleopatra

Q. This Shakespearean character's last words were "The rest is silence."   A. *Hamlet*

Q. Play set mainly in the Forest of Arden.   A. *As You Like It*

Q. Shakespearean character who proclaimed that he was "Ay, every inch a king."   A. *King Lear*

Q. Shakespearean play taken from Thomas Lodge's "Rosalynde: Euphues' Golden Legacie," its main character is Rosalind.   A. *As You Like It*

Q. It is thought that this play was written as a tribute to James I because of its flattering portrayal of how the Stuart line came to power.   A. *Macbeth*

Q. Shakespearean play that involves a Roman invasion of Britain.   A. *Cymbeline*

Q. Play centering on the twin sons of Aegeon.   A. *The Comedy of Errors*

Q. *The Comedy of Errors* is based on his *Menaechmi and Amphitruo.*   A. Plautus

Q. Both of the twins sons of Aegeon in *The Comedy of Errors* have this name.   A. Antipholus

Q. Both of the servants of the twin sons of Aegeon in *The Comedy of Errors* have this name.   A. Dromio

Q. In *The Comedy of Errors*, one of the twins lives in Ephesus, the other in this Sicilian city.   A. Syracuse

Q. Patrician Caius Martius was given this Shakespearean title name after winning the battle of Corioli.   A. Coriolanus

Q. Coriolanus was taken from this Greek biographer's *Lives*.
A. Plutarch

Q. This uncle of Hamlet poisoned his brother and supplied the poison that killed Hamlet, Laertes, and Gertrude.
A. Claudius

Q. Hamlet said of her, "Frailty, thy name is woman."
A. Gertrude

Q. Hamlet's girlfriend, she kills herself when Hamlet rejects her.   A. Ophelia

Q. The method of suicide chosen by Ophelia.   A. Drowning

Q. In his famous advice, Polonius states that "brevity is the soul of" this.   A. Wit

Q. Shakespearean character who says, "The lady doth protest too much, methinks."   A. Gertrude in *Hamlet*

Q. Hamlet died in his arms after being stabbed with a poisoned foil.   A. Horatio

Q. According to Hamlet, what deceased jester was "a fellow of infinite jest"?   A. Yorick

Q. In this Shakespearean play, Casca complained, "But for my own part, it was Greek to me."   A. *Julius Caesar*

Q. Shakespeare wrote two plays about the king of England who was originally named Henry Bolingbroke. What were his royal name and number?   A. *Henry IV*

Q. In *Henry IV*, Henry Percy, who had defeated the Scottish rebels but refused to surrender his prisoners to Henry IV, was given this nickname.   A. Hotspur

Q. At the end of *Henry IV, Part 2*, Prince Hal repudiates his misspent youth by banishing this self-indulgent braggart from his presence.   A. Sir John Falstaff

Q. Falstaff's death is given some attention in this play.
A. *Henry V*

Q. After hearing of the revolt by Hotspur, this character saves Henry IV's life and wins the Battle of Shrewsbury.
A. Prince Hal

Q. In Shakespeare's play, after his brother John of Lancaster defeated a Northumberland rebellion, Prince Hal became king with this name and number. A. *Henry V*

Q. *Henry V* contains what famous 1415 battle fought on St. Crispen's Day? A. Agincourt

Q. In *Henry VI*, when Dick the Butcher was contemplating what he'd do during a revolution he suggested this employment-based genocide. A. "Kill all the lawyers"

Q. Shakespearean trilogy of plays covering the Hundred Years War and the Wars of the Roses. A. *Henry VI*

Q. Shakespearean king who asked his troops to go, "once more unto the breach, dear friends, once more." A. Henry V

Q. True to form, this Shakespearean character rationalized, "The better part of valor is discretion." A. Falstaff

Q. Shakespearean play in which Falstaff says, "We have heard the chimes at midnight." A. Henry IV

Q. The last play performed at the Globe was this history play featuring a king and Cardinals Wolsey and Cranmer. A. Henry VIII

Q. In *Henry VIII*, what character says, "Had I but serv'd my God with half the zeal I served my king, he would not in mine age have left me naked to mine enemies." A. Thomas Wolsey

Q. After Wolsey refuses to condone the remarriage of Henry VIII, this man is appointed to do it. A. Cranmer

Q. In Shakespeare's *Julius Caesar,* he turns the Romans against the assassins with a stirring funeral speech. A. Marc Antony

Q. Cassius told Brutus, "The fault, dear Brutus, lies not in our stars, but in ourselves, that we are" these. A. Underlings

Q. According to Julius Caesar, this man had "a lean and hungry look." A. Cassius

Q. According to this wife of Caesar, "when beggars die, there are no comets seen; the heavens themselves blaze forth the death of princes." A. Calpurnia

Q. He said, "Cry 'Havoc' and let slip the dogs of war."
A. Marc Antony

Q. In this Shakespearean play a weak and despicable king fends off the royal claims of Arthur, duke of Brittany, but is poisoned in the end.   A. King John

Q. These two sisters in *King Lear* professed their love in the most grandiose and insincere terms.   A. Goneril and Regan

Q. In *King Lear*, she poisons her sister for the love of Edmund, the evil bastard son of Gloucester.   A. Goneril

Q. According to King Lear, "How sharper than a serpent's tooth it is to have" this.   A. A thankless child

Q. This Shakespearean title character was a patron of the arts whose erstwhile friends rejected him after rumors circulated that he was broke.   A. Timon of Athens

Q. This Shakespearean comedy concerns the king of Navarre and his courtiers who swear to eschew women for three years, but instead fall in love.   A. Love's Labour's Lost

Q. Already the thane of Glamis, when he learns that he is to become the thane of Cawdor, as predicted, his ambition is kindled.   A. Macbeth

Q. In *Macbeth*, the three witches tell this General that his sons will someday sit upon the throne.   A. Banquo

Q. Lady Macbeth urged her husband to kill this king.
A. Duncan

Q. Macbeth killed Duncan when he visited this castle, home of Macbeth.   A. Dunsinane

Q. The "Great Wood" that came against Dunsinane in *Macbeth*.   A. Great Birnam Wood

Q. After causing the death of Banquo, Macbeth caused the murder of the family of this man.   A. Macduff

Q. In this Shakespearean play, Vincentio deputizes Angelo to enforce Vienna's long-ignored laws, one of which bars cohabitation before marriage.   A. *Measure for Measure*

Q. Disguised as the lawyer Balthazar, she implored, "The quality of mercy is not strain'd."   A. Portia

Q. In The *Merchant of Venice*, Antonio takes a loan from Shylock in order to finance this friend's journey to win the hand of Portia. A. Bassanio

Q. He asked, "If you prick us, do we not bleed?" A. Shylock

Q. According to the Shakespearean title, they were Mrs. Ford and Mrs. Page. A. *The Merry Wives of Windsor*

Q. This play is set in Athens and the nearby woods. A. *A Midsummer Night's Dream*

Q. *A Midsummer Night's Dream* takes place as the wedding of this duke of Athens and this queen of the Amazons is planned. A. Theseus and Hippolyta

Q. Oberon, the king of the fairies in *A Midsummer Night's Dream*, begins the play extremely disgruntled with this wife. A. Titania

Q. Since this merry prankster uses his magic love juice indiscriminately, *A Midsummer Night's Dream* becomes a rather strange comedy. A. Puck (Robin Goodfellow)

Q. After Puck, in *A Midsummer Night's Dream*, gave Titania his magic love juice, she fell for this weaver whom Oberon had given the head of an ass. A. Bottom

Q. *The Murder of Gonzago* was performed within this Shakespearean play. A. *Hamlet*

Q. In *Much Ado About Nothing*, Claudio questions the virtue of this sister of Beatrice and rejects her at the altar. A. Hero

Q. This play is subtitled *The Moor of Venice*. A. *Othello*

Q. After this man was made Othello's chief lieutenant, Iago conspired to undo both the general and the lieutenant. A. Cassio

Q. According to Iago, Cassio was supposed to have had an illicit affair with this daughter of Brabantio. A. Desdemona

Q. Othello finally believed Iago's accusations when he found this article he had given Desdemona in Cassio's possession. A. Handkerchief

Q. Just before committing suicide, Othello asked to be remembered as one who "lov'd" this way. A. Not wisely but too well

Q. He warned Othello, "O! beware, my lord, of jealousy; it is the green-eyed monster." A. Iago

Q. In Othello, he was the "ancient" or ensign. A. Iago

Q. Shakespearean play about a prince who angered Antioch and was forced to wander about for years, losing a wife and daughter for a while. A. *Pericles, Prince of Tyre*

Q. This Shakespearean king called England a "precious stone set in the silver sea." A. *Richard II*

Q. In Shakespeare's play, after this man's death, Richard II confiscates his son's inheritance. A. John of Gaunt

Q. In Shakespeare's *Richard II*, he was the son of John of Gaunt who boldy invaded England from France, defeated the king, and became Henry IV. A. Henry Bolingbroke

Q. If you count the mention of his death in *Henry V,* he has been involved in more plays (four) than any other Shakespearean character. A. Falstaff

Q. This Shakespearean king died in battle at Bosworth Field in 1485. A. Richard III

Q. Elizabeth, whom Richard III wanted to marry in the play, and whom Henry VII married, was the daughter of this Yorkish king. A. Edward IV

Q. Because of the deadly feud between the Montagues and the Capulets, Romeo and Juliet are secretly married in the cell of this friar. A. Friar Laurence

Q. For killing this cousin of Juliet, Romeo is banished from Verona. A. Tybalt

Q. This friend of Romeo gives the famous Queen Mab speech, in which he calls her "the fairies' midwife." A. Mercutio

Q. The prologue to *Romeo and Juliet* describes them as a pair of these. A. Star-cross'd lovers

Q. In this play, Baptista refuses to allow Bianca to marry any of her suitors until her older sister can marry. A. *The Taming of the Shrew*

Q. He manages to tame Katharina by feigning indifference. A. Petruchio

Q. Before *The Tempest*'s Prospero was cast adrift, he had been duke of this city. A. Milan

Q. This Shakespearean character's brother, Alonso, the king of Naples, cast him and his daughter adrift on a bark; they were saved by Gonzalo. A. Prospero

Q. Raised without companions, this Shakespearean character is awestruck at seeing men, and says, "Oh, brave new world, that has such people in't." A. Miranda

Q. The son of Sycorax, a witch, and a devil, this supporting Shakespearean character symbolizes mankind's primitive urges. A. Caliban

Q. Prospero freed this sprite from a pine rift in which he was imprisoned by the evil witch Sycorax. A. Ariel

Q. Shakespearean king who lost twenty-one of twenty-five sons in wars, mostly against the Goths. A. Titus Andronicus

Q. This Shakespearean play is set during a truce between the Greeks and Trojans in the eighth year of the war. A. *Troilus and Cressida*

Q. In the Shakespearean play, Troilus disdains Cressida when he sees her give his love token to this mighty Greek warrior. A. Diomedes

Q. The title of this Shakespearean play refers to the date of Epiphany, when the social order would be reversed, lords wait on servants, etc. A. *Twelfth Night*

Q. This twin sister of Sebastian disguises herself as Cesario, the page of Duke Orsino, and falls in love with him. A. Viola

Q. The two Shakespearean plays that deal with shipwrecked, separated twins. A. *The Comedy of Errors* and *Twelfth Night*

Q. In this play, Proteus forgets his old love, Julia, and lies about his friend, Valentine, in order to win Sylvia. A. *Two Gentlemen of Verona*

Q. The title of this play on which Shakespeare collaborated around 1634, refers to two valiant Theban knights, Palamon and Arcite. A. *Two Noble Kinsmen*

Q. Leontes, king of Sicily, banishes his wife, abandons his daughter on some distant shore, but repents and gets both of them back in this play. A. *The Winter's Tale*

Q. This name of Leontes's lost daughter in *The Winter's Tale* literally means "lost little girl." A. Perdita

Q. "Exit, pursued by a bear" is a famed stage direction from this Shakespearean play. A. *The Winter's Tale*

Q. 1967's *The Chimes at Midnight,* by Orson Welles, was based on Shakespeare's play about this king. A. *Henry IV*

Q. Noted Japanese filmmaker Akira Kurosawa based *Throne of Blood* on this Shakespearean play. A. *Macbeth*

Q. Kurosawa's *Ran* is based on this Shakespearean play. A. *King Lear*

JOHN STEINBECK

The next three authors, John Steinbeck, Mark Twain, and Charles Dickens, are probably tied for second regarding how often they are the subject of *Jeopardy!* questions. But as in most categories, the writers will only ask you about the basics. Here they are:

Q. This Steinbeck story concerns Danny and his friends, Pillon, Pablo, Big Joe Portagee, and Old Pirate, who meet at Danny's house. A. *Tortilla Flat*

Q. This Steinbeck work deals with the struggles faced by migrant farm workers organizing into unions. A. *In Dubious Battle*

Q. This is what Lennie Small and George Milton dream of owning one day in *Of Mice and Men*. A. Farm

Q. The member of the Joad family who kills a man in *The Grapes of Wrath*. A. Tom Joad

Q. The sequel to this story was *Sweet Thursday*. A. *Cannery Row*

Q. This Steinbeck work is a rambling tale of people working at a fish factory. A. *Cannery Row*

Q. After Kino and Juana's baby in a Steinbeck work gets bitten by a scorpion, Kino finds one of these in the Gulf of California to pay a doctor. A. Pearl (in *The Pearl*)

Q. Adam Trask, the father of Cal and Aron, never forgives Cal for causing Aron's death in this Steinbeck novel. A. *East of Eden*

Q. Steinbeck title that could describe the vehicle involved in the movie *Speed*. A. *The Wayward Bus*

Q. In *Travels with Charley*, Charley was this type of dog. A. Poodle

Q. Steinbeck's *Cup of Gold* concerned this Central American buccaneer, who took over Nicaragua for a while. A. Henry Morgan

Q. Steinbeck's *The Long Valley* is a collection of short stories about this valley, where Steinbeck was born. A. Salinas

MARK TWAIN

Every *Jeopardy!* contestant should know that Mark Twain's real name was Samuel Langhorne Clemens, but a champion would know that he got his pen name from the call of Mississippi riverboatmen "sounding" the depth of the river with long poles. If the river was deep enough in a certain spot to cover two lines on their poles, they would yell out, "Mark Twain!" Here are some other bits of Twain trivia.

Q. Mark Twain was born in this town in Missouri, which shares its name with another state. A. Florida

Q. In 1853, after writing for newspapers in this Missouri city, Mark Twain left for St. Louis, Philadelphia, and New York. A. Hannibal

Q. In the 1860s Mark Twain was a journalist working for this western writer of *The Outcasts of Poker Flats*. A. Bret Harte

Q. In "The Celebrated Jumping Frog of Calaveras County," a miner named Jim Smiley bets that his frog, named this, could outjump any other. A. Dan'l Webster

Q. Though lecturing and short stories increased his reputation, Twain's place in the world of letters was ensured by this novel, a product of a European trip. A. *Innocents Abroad*

Q. Tom Sawyer and Huck Finn witness a murder because they are in the cemetery with a dead cat trying to cure these. A. Warts

Q. Muff Potter was accused of the murder in *Tom Sawyer*, but this character really did it. A. Injun Joe

Q. When Huck and Tom Sawyer run away to Jackson's Island, everyone believes them to be dead, including this aunt of Tom. A. Aunt Polly

Q. Tom Sawyer gets lost in a cave with this sweetheart but eventually escapes with buried treasure. A. Becky Thatcher

Q. Besides the *Adventures of Huckleberry Finn*, these were the other two sequels to *The Adventures of Tom Sawyer*. A. *Tom Sawyer, Detective* and *Tom Sawyer Abroad*

Q. The prince in *The Prince and the Pauper* eventually became this king. A. Edward VI

Q. While the prince wanders about in rags, this former pauper suffers the horrors of princedom in his stead. A. Tom Canty

Q. At the end of Huck Finn, Huck helps this runaway slave escape his captors. A. Jim

Q. A blow to the head conveys the superintendent of a Hartford arms factory back to medieval times in this Twain classic. A. *A Connecticut Yankee in King Arthur's Court*

Q. This Twain work is called a "tragedy" in its title. A. *The Tragedy of Pudd'nhead Wilson*

Q. This was the occupation of Pudd'nhead Wilson, who solves a murder and a case of mistaken identity in the Twain novel. A. Lawyer

Q. The mystery in this Twain novel revolves around two children, a mulatto and a white boy, born on the same day. A. *The Tragedy of Pudd'nhead Wilson*

Q. An unknown man "corrupted" this town by leaving a mysterious sack at a local bank and sending the secret phrase needed to claim it to nineteen prominent townsmen.
A. Hadleyburg

Q. After losing two daughters and his wife, Twain penned this bitter work in which Satan, disguised as a pleasing stranger, convinces a boy to kill a cripple.   A. *The Mysterious Stranger*

CHARLES DICKENS

Charles Dickens, when he first began writing, was a court clerk, and many of his works have to do with the legal system. He was also deeply influenced by his family's troubles with poverty, and works such as *Oliver Twist, David Copperfield,* and *Hard Times* expose the suffering of the poor in nineteenth-century England. Here are the most important things to know about Charles Dickens.

Q. Sidney Carton and Charles Darnay both loved this daughter of a wrongly imprisoned doctor in *A Tale of Two Cities.*
A. Lucie Manette

Q. This Dickens work was an indictment of the philosophical and practical attitudes that underlay nineteenth-century industrialism in England.   A. *Hard Times*

Q. The story of the two Gradgrind children whose grim, practical upbringing ruins their emotional futures.   A. *Hard Times*

Q. Though this vulgar banker in *Hard Times* claimed to have been poor, he was actually doted on by parents he pays to keep hidden.   A. Josiah Bounderby

Q. This serialized work was written as a series of letters from a travel club.   A. *Posthumous Papers of the Pickwick Club*

Q. An insult that sounds sincere but really is not is given this name derived from a Dickens work.   A. Pickwickian

Q. Monks is eventually discovered to be this Dickens title character's evil half-brother who was out to get all of their father's estate. A. *Oliver Twist*

Q. This official at Oliver Twist's workhouse gave his name to a term for the officious arrogance and conceit of petty dignitaries. A. Mr. Bumble

Q. Gruesome profession of Sowerberry, for whom Oliver Twist first worked after leaving the workhouse. A. Undertaker

Q. Though he assumed a suave and fawning manner, this leader of thieves was truly grasping and full of cruelty. A. Fagin

Q. Jack Dawkins, who perfected the art of picking pockets and petty thievery, was given this nickname. A. Artful Dodger

Q. The one redeeming feature of this violent housebreaker and murderer in *Oliver Twist* is that he likes his dog. A. Bill Sikes

Q. What Oliver Twist said about workhouses, this work said about schools, through the example of Dotheboys Hall. A. *Nicholas Nickleby*

Q. Mr. and Mrs. Wackford Squeers were corrupt, cruel schoolmasters at a school this title character attended. A. Nicholas Nickleby

Q. The Cheeryble brothers helped this main character. A. Nicholas Nickleby

Q. This Dickens work focused on the anti-Catholic Gordon Riots, which it argued were caused by a government heedless of its poor. A. *Barnaby Rudge*

Q. This half-witted title character carried around a large raven called Grip. A. Barnaby Rudge

Q. In this Dickens work, the main character's grandfather, a compulsive gambler, loses the store to Quilp. A. *The Old Curiosity Shop*

Q. Little Nell's last name. A. Trent

Q. When Little Nell and her grandfather worked for a kind schoolmaster, Little Nell supported them by doing this at a nearby church. A. Tending graves

Q. The title of this Dickens work describes John Harmon, who will receive an inheritance if he marries Bella Wilfers.
A. *Our Mutual Friend*

Q. Abel Magwitch was this Dickens character's secret benefactor, until discovered to be a convict. A. Pip, or Philip Pirrip

Q. This Dickens spinster was jilted at the altar and thus hated all men. A. Miss Havisham

Q. When Philip Pirrip heard that he had a secret benefactor, he left his genuine friends behind and left for London to fulfill all of his... A. *Great Expectations*

Q. Young lady that Miss Havisham turned against all men in *Great Expectations*. A. Estella

Q. After her debt-ridden family suddenly receives a great fortune, Amy—given this title nickname—is the only one who remains genuinely nice. A. *Little Dorrit*

Q. This Dickens novel attacked bureaucracy and the practice of imprisonment for debt. A. *Little Dorrit*

Q. In *Little Dorrit*, Amy's future husband spends years fighting the bureaucracy in this aptly named office. A. Office of Circumlocution

Q. Nine members of this family of bumbling incompetent goverment officials, most notably Tite, appear in *Little Dorrit*. A. Barnacle

Q. The lingering question in this Dickens work is whether the title character is really still alive, is Mr. Datchery, or was killed by Jasper or Neville. A. *The Mystery of Edwin Drood*

Q. The chapters of this Dickens book that take place in America attacked American provincialism and offended many Americans. A. *Martin Chuzzlewit*

Q. The daughters of this canting hypocrite, a Dickens title character, were named Charity and Mercy. A. Martin Chuzzlewit

Q. A large, badly rolled cotton umbrella has come to be known as this, named for a drink-sodden, low-class nurse from *Martin Chuzzlewit*. A. Gamp (from Sarah Gamp)

Q. The title character of this Christmas tale by Dickens makes
noise when all is well and is silent when all is not well.
A. *The Cricket on the Hearth*

Q. This Dickens work is an exposé of corruption and court delay. A. *Bleak House*

Q. This title refers to the lonely estate of Mr. Jarndyce.
A. *Bleak House*

Q. This Dickens work contains the multigenerational case of
Jarndyce v. Jarndyce. A. *Bleak House*

Q. All the main character in this Dickens work ever wanted
was a son to add to the firm's name. A. *Dombey and Son*

Q. According to Dickens, which of his works, an indictment of
the treatment of children in the nineteenth century, was
his "favorite child"? A. *David Copperfield*

Q. This poor old man with a good heart helped David Copperfield. A. Mr. Micawber

Q. This David Copperfield villain's name is now synonymous
with ruthless ambition cloaked in humility. A. Uriah
Heep

Q. While Dickens sometimes went by "Boz," his illustrator
went by this similar-sounding name. A. Phiz (a.k.a. Hablot
K. Browne)

CHAPTER 14

The Finer Things in Life

Sometimes, when people ask me how I knew the things I knew on the show, I tell them that it was from living "the *Jeopardy!* lifestyle." A few think that means studying all the time, but true fans of the show will know that *Jeopardy!* wants to show that their contestants are well rounded and interested in the finer things in life. This chapter delves into some of the finer things that you might be able to buy more of if you win on the show.

SOURCES OF QUICK INFORMATION

The Art of Mixing Drinks, David A. Embury (Garden City, NY: Doubleday, 1961)

The Ultimate Wine Book, Don and Betty Martin (Columbia, CA: Pine Cone Press, 1993)

Potent Potables

Studying for this category can really make it hard to study for all the rest, if you know what I mean. And people will ask you lots of embarrassing questions if you answer all the questions in this category. In fact, when I knew the two ingredients in a Cape

Codder, Alex asked me how I knew that. I responded, "Oh...no reason...." The reason I did know, however, is that I read *The Art of Mixing Drinks* and the section of the *New York Public Library Desk Reference* on "Alcoholic Drink Recipes" (p. 600).

THE HARD STUFF

Any hard-drinking southerner will tell you to start with the hard stuff if you plan a night of mixed drinking. As they put it, "Wine then liquor, you'll be sicker. Liquor then wine, you'll be fine." Heeding that warning, we are going to start with questions about whiskey and other hard liquor. See how many you get.

Q. While this 100-proof liquor's formula is supposedly secret, it tastes like a peach-flavored bourbon.   A. Southern Comfort

Q. The Danish variety of this caraway-flavored liquor is both the driest and most famous.   A. Aquavit

Q. Liquor made from the maguey plant, a species of aloe grown extensively in Mexico.   A. Tequila

Q. There are three varieties of this liquor: Geneva, London, and sloe.   A. Gin

Q. Arrack and Okolehao are native liquors from this U.S. state.   A. Hawaii

Q. V.V.S.O.P. on a bottle of this indicates that it is very, very old.   A. Brandy

Q. Johnnie Walker Black and Chivas Regal are examples of this liquor.   A. Scotch whisky

Q. A Tom Collins is not really a Tom Collins unless it contains the Old Tom variety of this liquor.   A. Gin

Q. Its most general definition is any spiritous liquor made from grain.   A. Whiskey

Q. Any liquor made from fruit.   A. Brandy

Q. Simply put, it's the product of fermenting sugar.   A. Rum

Q. Remy Martin, Monnet, Marie Brizard, and Courvoisier are all types of this brandy.   A. Cognac

GIN

Q. Not really a gin at all, it is a liqueur made of a berry from the blackthorn or juniper plant. A. Sloe Gin

Q. Country where the best gin was originally made. A. Holland

Q. To make gin, raw alcohol is placed with bark, seeds, roots, and these berries into a still and is distilled again. A. Juniper

WHISKEY

Q. Grain that forms the basis of bourbon whiskey. A. Corn

Q. Scotch whiskey's characteristic smoky taste results from the barley malt being dried over fires fueled by this. A. Peat

Q. Fulstrength, made by the Drambuie firm, is often considered the finest whiskey from this country. A. Scotland

Q. Erin's Antique, John Jameson, and Bushmills are whiskeys from this country. A. Ireland

Q. V.O. and Pedigree are types of whiskeys made by this Canadian company. A. Seagram's

Q. This process of making bourbon uses less corn and more barley malt than the sweet mash process. A. Sour mash

Q. If a whiskey is this, nothing has been added to it but pure distilled water. A. Bonded

Q. While Kentucky is famous for bourbon whiskey, this state is famous for its ryes. A. Pennsylvania

Q. Colorful name given to green Kentucky whiskey straight from the still. A. White mule

RUM

Q. While rum can be made from the fermented juice of the entire sugar cane, for the most part it is made from this heavy, dark syrup by-product. A. Molasses

Q. Batavia arak, made from molasses from this Indonesian island mixed with red rice, is a form of rum used a great deal in the Netherlands and Scandinavia. A. Java

Q. Because it has a more subdued flavor, rum from this island should be used as a cocktail base while the Jamaican variety makes a better flavoring agent. A. Cuba

Q. Home island of Bacardi, Carioca, and Ronrico rums. A. Puerto Rico

Q. Demerara rums are made from sugar produced in the Demerara River section of this former British colony in South America. A. Guyana (formerly British Guiana)

BRANDY

Q. This finest grape brandy in the world comes exclusively from a French district lying along the Charente River, not far from Bordeaux. A. Cognac

Q. This French brandy is often considered a close second to cognac. A. Armagnac

Q. Kirsch is brandy made by distilling them. A. Cherries

Q. Slivovitz, quetsch, and mirabelle brandies are made by distilling these. A. Plums

Q. Framboise is made by distilling these. A. Raspberries

Q. An Italian brandy made with the last press of the grapes. A. Grappa

Q. Pisco is a grape brandy that comes from this South American country. A. Peru

Q. Fundador is a brandy made in this country. A. Spain

Q. This Greek brandy is a satisfactory cocktail substitute for cognac because it lacks the sweet sherry flavor of Spanish brandies. A. Metaxa

LIGHTER LIQUORS

Well, if you are still standing after these last quizzes, try these questions about some gentler libations.

POPULAR DRINKS AND WHAT'S IN THEM

Gin Drinks	*What is added besides the main alcoholic ingredient*
Bronx Cocktail	dry and sweet vermouth, orange juice
Gibson	dry vermouth, pearl onion
Gimlet	lime juice
Gin Fizz	lemon juice, powdered sugar, soda water
Martini	dry vermouth, olive (or lemon twist)
Orange Blossom	orange juice
Rickey	lime juice, soda water
Salty Dog	grapefruit juice, salt
Singapore Sling	see Brandy section
Tom Collins	lemon juice, powdered sugar, soda water
White Lady	powdered sugar, cream, egg white

Brandy Drinks	
Alexander	crème de cacao, cream
B & B	benedictine
Sidecar	Cointreau or Triple Sec, lemon juice
Singapore Sling	gin, cherry brandy, lemon juice, powdered sugar, soda water
Stinger	white crème de menthe

Rum Drinks	
Cuba Libre	Coke and lime juice
Daiquiri	lime juice, powdered sugar, crushed fruit
Mai Tai	curaçao, lime juice, grenadine, almond-flavored syrup, powdered sugar
Pina Colada	light and dark rum; orange, lime, and pineapple juice; grenadine; coconut milk
Planter's Punch	soda water, lime juice, powdered sugar, angostura bitters
Zombie	apricot brandy; pineapple, lime, and orange juice; powdered sugar

Vodka Drinks	
Black Russian	Kahlua
Bloody Mary	tomato juice, lemon juice, Worcestershire, Tabasco, celery salt
Screwdriver	orange juice

Harvey Wallbanger   orange juice and Galliano

Whiskey Drinks

Manhattan   vermouth, angostura bitters, maraschino
                      cherry
Rob Roy   A Manhattan with Scotch whisky
Mint Julep   4 sprigs mint, water, lump of sugar,
                      crushed ice
Old-fashioned   1/2 lump sugar, angostura bitters, water (in
                      short glass)
Rusty Nail   Scotch whisky with Drambuie
7 & 7   Seagram's whiskey and 7-Up
Whiskey Sour   lemon juice, powdered sugar

Other

Black Velvet   Guinness stout and champagne
Grasshopper   Crème de menthe, white crème de cacao,
                      cream
Margarita   Cointreau or Triple Sec, lime juice, salt-
                      rimmed glass
Tequila Sunrise   orange juice, grenadine (not stirred)
Toddy   (brandy, gin, rum, or whiskey) add sugar
                      and water

Q. Babylonian law decreed that the bride must keep the groom
   supplied with this wine for a month after the wedding.
   A. Mead

Q. This is the term for any liquor, especially rum, that has
   been diluted with water.   A. Grog

Q. After mashing apples, you get the sweet variety of this; after
   you let that ferment, you get the hard variety.   A. Cider

Q. Because an ingredient in it, wormwood, was considered
   habit forming and insanity-causing, it has been banned in
   several countries.   A. Absinthe

Q. Dark brown beer named for the type of manual laborers
   who would drink it.   A. Porter

Q. The Guinness company made this stronger, more heavily
   hopped version of porter famous.   A. Stout

Q. The French, rather than Italian, type of this makes a better gin martini.   A. Vermouth

FORTIFIED WINES

Q. Though sherries are made around the world, this country makes the finest.   A. Spain

Q. A sweet, red fortified wine from Oporto, Portugal.   A. Port

Q. Solera is the mother wine that is at the heart of this Spanish fortified wine.   A. Port

Q. As a dessert wine, this brand of sherry is the king of them all.   A. Harvey's Bristol Cream

Q. This spirit is made by halting the fermentation process two-thirds of the way through by the addition of Portuguese brandy.   A. Port

Q. This dark, sweet, heavy fortified wine has no real use except in cooking, where it serves somewhat the same purpose as sherry but with a different taste.   A. Marsala

Q. The finos (light, dry) variety is popular in England, while the olorosos variety is known in America.   A. Sherry

Q. What was the medium-dry variety of sherry that was made famous by Poe?   A. Amontillado

Q. The tawny variety of this spirit loses color each time it's fired in order to remove the crusty sediment that forms on the wood cask it's stored in.   A. Port

EQUIPMENT AND ADDITIVES

A martini is hardly worth indulging in if you don't have a properly chilled martini glass. See what you know about these other essential items in any well-stocked wet bar.

Q. What glasses sound like they've gone out of style?   A. Old-fashioneds

Q. A straight-sided glass shaped like a cordial glass but about twice as high, holding $1\frac{1}{2}$ to 2 ounces.   A. Pousse-café glass

Q. A 1-ounce whiskey glass is given this equine name.
A. Pony

Q. Also called simply "a drink," it's a 3-ounce whiskey glass.
A. Jigger

Q. What is the term for the smallest, and apparently politest, type of liquor glass?   A. Cordial

Q. Glass that gets its name because it allows the user to sniff the brandy.   A. Snifter or inhaler

Q. Required with juleps and similar tall iced drinks such as daiquiris, it should never be used with any other cocktail.
A. Straw

Q. Despite the name, they actually tend to smooth out the taste of a drink by removing an acrid whiskey taste.
A. Bitters

Q. It is a popular almond-flavored nonalcoholic syrup used in cocktail-making.   A. Orgeat

Q. What perpetually teased mythological character gave his name to a lockable, cagelike container for displaying bottles or decanters of wine or spirits?   A. Tantalus

Fashion, Clothes, and Fabrics

Have you noticed how much the world of high fashion has suddenly come into the limelight? Three times a day, VH1, E!, and CNN have a segment on fashion. VH1 even hosts The Fashion Awards. *Jeopardy!* also has been showing increased interest in this topic, whether it's "Fashion" or "Fabrics" or even as part of the favorite category "Hints from Heloise."

THE WORLD OF FASHION QUIZ

Q. What French woman designer was the first to put women in pants?   A. Coco Chanel

Q. Who is the German designer behind the fashion houses of Chloe and Chanel these days?   A. Karl Lagerfeld

Q. Tom Ford, a Texan, has turned around the fortunes of what fashion house?   A. Gucci

Q. What son of Russian and Italian parents created Jackie O's look when she was first lady? A. Oleg Cassini

Q. What distinctive designer created the costumes for the films *Funny Face* and *Breakfast at Tiffany's*? A. Hubert Givenchy

Q. What was the famous nickname of the model who was "the Face of 1966"? A. Twiggy

Q. What street in London is associated with women's fashion? A. Carnaby Street

Q. From French for "sewing," it's the business of designing and creating fashion. A. Couture

Q. This loom was operated by a chain of variously perforated cards. A. Jacquard

Q. The DK in DKNY is for her. A. Donna Karan

Q. She was born Diane Michelle Halfin in Brussels, and her jersey wrap dress is making a comeback. A. Diane von Fürstenberg

Q. This street in London is associated with fine men's apparel. A. Saville Row

CLOTHES

Q. What word can mean your friends or the leather leggings for gauchos? A. Chaps

Q. What above-the-ankle pants with tapered legs are named for a Greek Island? A. Capri pants

Q. What word, taken from the Malay for "cloth covering," describes the loosely fitting wrap dress made famous by Dorothy Lamour? A. Sarong

Q. It's a jacket like the one a matador wears; go ask Bo Derek. A. Bolero

Q. Undergarment stiffened with whalebone and resembling a corset. A. Bodice

Q. Originally a garment worn while combing the hair, it now describes a woman's loose negligee or dressing gown. A. Peignoir

Q. It's a hard leather shoe from Scotland or a thick accent.
A. Brogue

Q. A piece of cloth five to seven feet long that is wrapped around the head or shoulders, then around the waist to form a skirt. A. Sari

FABRICS

Q. What stretchy Dupont fiber is used to give tightness and form to control-top features? A. Lycra

Q. TV's Matlock wore suits of this puckered material with tiny blue vertical stripes. A. Seersucker

Q. "Matte" means a color or fabric without this. A. Shine or gloss

Q. This light, delicate plainweave fabric takes its name from the French for "rag." A. Chiffon

Q. Taking its name from the French for "caterpillar," it is a yarn with pile protruding all around. A. Chenille

Q. As a general term, it refers to a mutant type of animal in which the length and silkiness of the coat are much greater than in the wild. A. Angora

Q. This branch of the Scottish clan Campbell is now famous for its distinctive tartan. A. Argyle

Q. What checkered fabric takes its name from the Malay language for "checkered cloth"? A. Gingham

Q. What is the general term in fashion for any materials pasted onto fabric? A. Appliqué

Q. What smooth, crisp plainwoven fabric is associated with prom dresses? A. Taffeta

Q. What thin crinkly fabric, which shares its name with a breakfast food, is made by stressing fabric with caustic soda? A. Crepe

Q. What fabric, often used in men's jackets, is made from the wool of the Angora goat? A. Mohair

Q. This fine, soft wool is made from the Kashmir goat.
A. Cashmere

Q. What fabric can measure up to twenty-two wales per inch? *A.* Corduroy

Q. This fabric takes its name from the Persian *shir-o-shakar,* meaning "milk and sugar," and has alternating stripes of puckered and flat cloth. *A.* Seersucker

Q. This Moroccan crepe fabric's name is almost an anagram of that country. *A.* Marocain

Q. This is a plainwoven or twilled silk usually printed with a neat, evenly spaced pattern. *A.* Foulard

Q. From the French for "double thread," it is a basic textile weave that produces diagonal patterns. *A.* Twill

Q. This thin, often see-through, woven fabric probably originated in Gaza, hence the name. *A.* Gauze

Q. Taken from the French for "goose summer," it is an extremely thin, gauzelike fabric. *A.* Gossamer

Q. This firm, durable fabric has a steep twill, forming distinct diagonal ribs. In a Simon and Garfunkel song, the man in a suit made of it was a spy. *A.* Gabardine

Q. It is a brocade made with tinsel filling threads, often gold or silver. *A.* Lamé

Q. The sikkah, an Arabic stamped coin, eventually gave its name to what small bit of metal stuck to a dress? *A.* Sequin

Q. A fabric used to cover books, it is named for a city in northern Iraq where it was made. *A.* Muslin

Q. Literally, what shiny, rubberlike clothing material means "new rubber"? *A.* Neoprene

Gems and Jewels

Jewels have occupied an amazing place in mankind's history and are universally revered by all cultures. *Jeopardy!* uses this category rather frequently, so you should start by memorizing the birthstones.

Q. It is said that this gem's luster will be revealed even if the stone is hidden beneath thick clothing. *A.* Ruby

Q. Some believed that this blue gem, praised for its beauty and coolness to the touch, could put out fires; some still believe it promotes clear thinking. A. Sapphire

Q. April must be the king of the months, because it has this, the king of gems, as its birthstone. A. Diamond

Q. Gem that might be named for a pomegranate, whose seeds it resembles. A. Garnet

Q. Possibly representing the new green shoots of spring, this is May's birthstone. A. Emerald

Q. Both of these August birthstones are associated with the sun. A. Peridot, sardonyx

Q. This usually violet gem takes its name from the Greek for "without drunkenness," because it was reputed to protect its wearer from intoxication. A. Amethyst

Q. Gem whose name is from the Latin for "seawater." A. Aquamarine

Q. Although aquamarine is the traditioinal March birthstone, this gem, also called heliotrope, meaning "sun-turning," is sometimes used. A. Bloodstone

Q. Wealthy parents in India would sprinkle tiny ones over the heads of infants to keep them pure and innocent. A. Diamonds

Q. The rich green of this gem is said to symbolize new life. A. Emerald

Q. According to legend, Noah used one of these red gems to light his ark. A. Garnet

Q. Sudden changes in temperature can cause its fragile surface to shatter, which led to the superstition that wearing it may bring bad luck. A. Opal

Q. Its shape and luminosity explain its designation as gem of the moon. A. Pearl

Q. This yellow-green gem, a birthstone for August, is called the gem of the sun. A. Peridot

Q. This other August birthstone has alternating black and white markings, which are said to symbolize the sun and moon. A. Sardonyx

Q. The Greeks believed this yellow gem, named for an island in the Red Sea, guarded against calamity. A. Topaz

Q. This gem, supposed to bring prosperity, takes its name from the French word for "Turkish." A. Turquoise

Q. This golden-yellow gem sounds like a fruit related to lemons or limes. A. Citrine

Q. This blue-purple gem is found mainly in the East African country for which it is named. A. Tanzanite

Q. This gem, which is different colors in natural and artificial light, was discovered in the 1880s in the Ural Mountains and named for the leader of the discoverer's nation. A. Alexandrite

Money and Riches

This section is particularly appropriate in a book about *Jeopardy!* I mean, winning money is what it is all about, isn't it? See what you know.

ENGLISH MONEY

Q. An English pound was made up of one pound of these, so named because a little star was stamped on each. A. Sterlings

Q. This one-pound coin was given a name that was a synonym for the queen or king. A. Sovereign

Q. This symbol comes from the first letter of the Latin word *librum*, "crossed." A. Pound sign

Q. This four-letter word is the Latin-sounding nickname for a pound. A. Quid

Q. Before England standardized its currency, twenty of these made up a pound. A. Shilling

Q. This three-letter word is the boyish nickname for a shilling. A. Bob

Q. This was the plural of "penny" in the old English coinage system. A. Pence

Q. Twelve of these coins made up a shilling under the old English coinage system. A. Pence

Q. This British unit of currency was originally a coin with an elephant stamped on it and made from gold from a certain area of Africa, hence its name. A. Guinea

Q. This unit of the old English currency is equivalent to one pound plus one shilling. A. Guinea

Q. This silver coin formerly used in England and still used in Holland is so named because it had a flower on it. A. Florin

Q. The silver coin worth five shillings was named for an accoutrement of the king. A. Crown

Q. This tiny amount was equivalent to a quarter of a penny under the old English coinage system. A. Farthing

THE RICHEST OF THE RICH

Q. This Augsburg merchant first cornered the copper market and then became banker to kings, emperors, and popes.
A. Jakob Fugger

Q. This financier was nicknamed "the Commodore." A. Cornelius Vanderbilt

Q. Because he bragged that his estate rivaled that of the king, this finance minister to Louis XIV was convicted of embezzling state funds. A. Nicolas Fouquet

Q. For whom was the Central University of Nashville renamed? A. Cornelius Vanderbilt

Q. What method of transportation earned Cornelius Vanderbilt his fortune? A. Steamboats

Q. What miserly millionairess refused to pay for medical treatment for her son at Bellevue, causing his leg to be amputated? A. Hetty Green

Q. What billionaire started out by selling grain, hay, and meats on the Cleveland docks? A. John D. Rockefeller

Q. Who founded the Standard Oil Company? A. John D. Rockefeller

Q. What great industrialist formerly was a chief engineer for the Edison Illuminating Company?   A. Henry Ford

Q. What ex–cotton farmer made a fortune in oil?   A. H. I. Hunt

Q. Who said in 1957, "A billion dollars isn't what it used to be"?   A. J. P. Getty

Q. What son of an Oklahoma oilman made billions off his deal with Ibn-Saud of Saudi Arabia?   A. J. P. Getty

Q. Who owned Citizens Bank and Bankers Life Insurance Company?   A. John Macarthur

Q. What "Golden Greek" owned a yacht called the *Christina*?   A. Aristotle Onassis

CHAPTER 15

Jeopardy! Specialties

One of my major goals in writing this book was to provide information that *Jeopardy!* always asks about but you can't easily find in one place. It took me months and half a dozen sources to compile this information about holidays, the calendar, and national parks. But it was worth it, for at least five questions came up in the Tournament of Champions that I knew just because I wrote these questions preparing for the show. You get to learn all the same facts without all the trouble.

Holidays and Observances

Did you know that the expression "red-letter days" comes from the fact that calendars used to have the holidays printed in red ink? That is just one of the many calendar- and holiday-related facts that *Jeopardy!* loves to ask about. Now that you've bought this book, you can take these four holiday quizzes. Then you will be an expert in anything *Jeopardy!* can throw at you.

CHRISTIAN HOLIDAYS QUIZ

Q. What is the first day of Lent, and also the name of a work by T. S. Eliot? A. Ash Wednesday

Q. What do Christians call the Sunday before Easter, commemorating Jesus' entry into Jerusalem? A. Palm Sunday

Q. Many worshipers begin Easter with a sunrise service to follow the example of what woman, who went to Christ's tomb "early while it was yet dark"? A. Mary Magdalen

Q. The medieval practice of parishioners dressing as saints and angels and parading through the courtyard explains some of the practice on what holiday? A. Halloween

Q. Originally a day of penance, what last day before Lent is now usually spent in exuberant feasting? A. Fat Tuesday (also known as Shrove Tuesday or Mardi Gras)

Q. Full observance of what holy day actually lasts from Septuagesima Sunday, seventy days before it, to Pentecost, fifty days after it? A. Easter

Q. What word, which is part of the ecclesiastical name for Mardi Gras, is a form of a verb that means "to forgive sins"? A. Shrove

Q. What holy day marks the date of Christ's crucifixion? A. Good Friday

Q. What is the end of the full ecclesiastical celebration of Easter? A. Pentecost

Q. What Christian holiday celebrates the descent of the Holy Spirit upon the Apostles? A. Pentecost

Q. What Christian holiday marks the day on which Gabriel informed Mary that she would give birth to Jesus? A. Annunciation Day

Q. What is the period of expectation and preparation that begins on the Sunday closest to November 30 called in the Catholic church? A. Advent

Q. Formerly the principal feast of the church year, it celebrates the presence of the body of Christ in the Eucharist. What is this feast day, also a Texas city? A. Corpus Christi

Q. In America, many churches mark the Sunday nearest this holy day as a day to pay tribute to those who have died the previous year. What holy day is it? A. All Saints Day

Q. What name for Holy Thursday comes from the "mandate" that Christ gave to his disciples at the Last Supper?
A. Maundy Thursday

Q. When Jesus entered Jerusalem in triumph, what were spread before him to honor him? A. Palm fronds

Q. What Christian holiday, about twelve days after Christmas, commemorates the wise men's visit to the Christ child?
A. Epiphany

Q. What name is given the Sunday after Pentecost, which honors the union of the Father, Son, and Holy Spirit?
A. Trinity Sunday

Q. Because the "forty days" in this period does not include Sundays, there are actually forty-six calendar days between Ash Wednesday and Easter. What is it? A. Lent

Q. What Christian holiday is also called Whitsunday? A. Pentecost

JEWISH HOLIDAYS

Q. What Jewish holiday is also called the Day of Judgment and Remembrance? A. Rosh Hashanah

Q. Originally an agricultural festival, what Jewish "Feast of Weeks" celebrates the revelation of the Torah at Mt. Sinai? A. Shavuoth

Q. The Jewish Sabbath starts on sundown on what day?
A. Friday

Q. Jewish families take their meals in crudely constructed booths during what harvest festival, associated with Thanksgiving? A. Sukkoth

Q. Blown on Rosh Hashanah, a shofar is an elaborately decorated what? A. Ram's Horn

Q. What is the Jewish holiday celebrating an everlasting lampful of oil in the Temple? A. Hanukkah

Q. On what Jewish holiday is a goat released into the desert to carry away all sins? A. Yom Kippur

Q. What Jewish holiday is considered to be the Birthday of the World? A. Rosh Hashanah

Q. What Jewish holiday is also known as the Feast of Dedication? A. Hanukkah

Q. What Jewish observance begins with the reading of the Kol Nidre, which nullifies unfulfilled vows of the preceding year? A. Yom Kippur

Q. What Jewish holiday is also called the Day of Atonement? A. Yom Kippur

Q. What is the special dinner celebration associated with Passover called? A. Seder

Q. Children celebrate this holiday commemorating the undoing of Haman's plot to murder all Persian Jews, by dressing up in costumes. A. Purim

Q. What Jewish holiday is also known as Pesach? A. Passover

Q. The name of this Jewish holiday could be translated from Hebrew as "Head of the World." A. Rosh Hashanah

THE ONLY THREE ISLAMIC CALENDAR QUESTIONS THAT COME UP

Q. What is the holy day of the weekly Islamic calendar? A. Friday or Jumuah

Q. What is the famous Ninth Month of the Islamic calendar? A. Ramadan

Q. Years in the Gregorian calendar are denominated a.d., meaning "year of the lord." Years in the Muslim calendar are designated a.h., meaning years after what? A. Hejira, which was Mohammed's journey to Mecca

NONRELIGIOUS HOLIDAYS QUIZ

Q. What is always the first Tuesday after the first Monday in November? A. Election Day

Q. What holiday was first celebrated in 1877, one hundred years after the resolution that adopted the present design of Old Glory? *A.* Flag Day

Q. The third Saturday in May, it commemorates all American soldiers. What holiday is it? *A.* Armed Forces Day

Q. First observed in 1952, this little-known holiday falls on the same day—September 17—as Constitution Day, which it replaced as a holiday. *A.* Citizenship Day

Q. What month does Father's Day fall in? *A.* June

Q. What holiday was first observed in West Virginia in 1908, though it was not until 1972 that Richard Nixon designated its official observance? *A.* Father's Day

Q. February 15 commemorates what cofounder and later president of the National Woman Suffrage Association? *A.* Susan B. Anthony

Q. National Maritime Day commemorates the departure of what ship, the first steam-powered vessel to successfully cross the Atlantic? *A.* S.S. *Savannah*

Q. Which holiday falls on November 11, commemorating the "11th hour of the 11th day of the 11th month"? *A.* Veteran's Day

Q. What country finally adopted the Gregorian calendar in 1752? *A.* England

Q. Internationally, Arbor Day is celebrated December 22; in the U.S., it is celebrated on the last Friday in what month? *A.* April

Q. A holiday on October 24 commemorates the ratification of what international document on October 24, 1945? *A.* United Nations Charter

Q. In the Middle Ages, many believed this date was the one on which birds picked their mates. *A.* February 14

Q. What holiday, the idea of Peter J. McGuire, president of the United Brotherhood of Carpenters and Joiners of America, was officially recognized in 1894? *A.* Labor Day

Q. Before 1954, Veteran's Day was known as what? *A.* Armistice Day

Q. Conceived by Anne M. Jarvis in Philadelphia, this was declared an official observance in 1914. A. Mother's Day

Q. Whose memory is celebrated the third Monday in January? A. Martin Luther King Jr.

Q. What U.S. holiday is celebrated on the third Monday in February? A. Presidents Day

Q. What holiday was proclaimed by Abraham Lincoln in 1863? A. Thanksgiving

Q. What U.S. holiday is always celebrated on the last Monday in May? A. Memorial Day

Q. What holiday was first celebrated in October 1792, three hundred years after the event it commemorates? A. Columbus Day

Q. Dating from the Civil War, what holiday used to be known as Decoration Day? A. Memorial Day

Q. Whose day is the second Monday in October? A. Columbus Day

Q. What holiday always falls on the first Monday in September? A. Labor Day

Q. You might want to buy an apple or two to honor these people on the Tuesday of the first full week of May. Who are they? A. Teachers

Q. What holiday always falls on the fourth Thursday in November? A. Thanksgiving

NATIONAL PARKS QUIZ

Theodore Roosevelt started the national park movement when he named Devil's Tower as a national monument. Like Richard Dreyfuss in the movie *Close Encounters of the Third Kind,* Americans have since been drawn to national parks by the millions. See how much you know.

Q. Located on Bar Harbor, this national park contains the highest point on the Atlantic Coast. A. Acadia

Q. The Colorado River also cuts a gorge through this national park located near Moab, Utah, which contains many huge rock formations formed by erosion. A. Arches

Q. This national park contains the Pine Ridge Indian reservation near the site of the Wounded Knee battleground. A. Badlands

Q. You can see a dramatic array of U.S. and Mexican flowers in this national park located in Texas. A. Big Bend

Q. Underwater coral reefs and marine life are the major attractions of this national park located in Homestead, Florida. A. Biscayne

Q. Bryce Canyon National Park, with its multicolored rock erosions, is located in this western state. A. Utah

Q. Capitol Reef National Park is not underwater; instead, it includes colorful rock formations around Torrey, in this state. A. Utah

Q. Though this New Mexico park features an impressive array of desert plants on the surface, the main attraction is the vast caves below. A. Carlsbad Caverns

Q. Marine life and sea birds are the main attractions in this national park located off the coast of Ventura, California. A. Channel Islands

Q. This national recreation area, noted for its mineral springs, is located outside Sulphur, Oklahoma. A. Chickasaw National Recreation Area

Q. This national park contains the deepest lake (2,000 feet) in the U.S. A. Crater Lake

Q. Mangrove swamps make up most of the immense subtropical wilderness of this Florida national park. A. Everglades

Q. This Alaskan national park contains the Great Mendenhall Glacier and is near Mount Logan, the highest point in Canada. A. Glacier Bay

Q. The gates of the Arctic National Park and Reserve open up to this mountain range, north of the Arctic Circle. A. Brooks Range

Q. Ancient Blackfoot hunting grounds are featured in this Montana national park. A. Glacier

Q. Along with Glacier National Park, this Canadian park makes up an International Peace Park, founded in 1932. A. Waterton

Q. The Havasupai Indian reservation is located deep within this Arizona national park. A. Grand Canyon

Q. You can trace the footsteps of many famous explorers in this national park located in Moose, Wyoming. A. Grand Teton

Q. This National Park, headquartered in Gatlinburg, Tennessee, contains the highest mountains in the eastern United States. A. Great Smoky Mountains National Park

Q. The highest point in Texas is located in this national park. A. Guadalupe Mountains National Park

Q. Haleakala National Park, which contains a famous crater and rare semitropical wildlife, is located near Makawao on this Hawaiian island. A. Maui

Q. You have to go to this island to see Hawaii Volcanoes National Park, containing Kilauea and Mauna Loa. A. Hawaii

Q. You can visit historic fisheries and pre-Columbian copper mines in this Michigan National Park, located in Lake Superior. A. Isle Royale

Q. Katmai National Park in Alaska features the mysterious and beautiful Valley of Ten Thousand of these. A. Smokes

Q. Located near Seward, Alaska, this national park contains ice fields and numerous breathtaking fjords. A. Kenai Fjords

Q. Kings Canyon National Park features a mile-deep canyon cut into the Sierras in this state. A. California

Q. Cook Inlet, part of Lake Clark National Park, is located near this Alaskan city. A. Anchorage

Q. This live volcano in Mineral, California, which last erupted in 1921, gave its name to a national park. A. Mt. Lassen (Lassen Volcanic National Park)

Q. Mesa Verde National Park, home to spectacular pre-Columbian cliff dwellings, is located in this state. A. Colorado

Q. Only experienced mountaineers are allowed to attempt a climb to the summit of this 14,410-foot mountain in Washington. A. Mt. Rainier

Q. Located in Sedro Wooley, Washington, this national park features an Alpine wilderness in the range for which it's named. A. North Cascades

Q. A rainforest of giant evergreens, mountains, and rocky beaches make up this national park located on the peninsula between the Pacific Ocean and Puget Sound. A. Olympic

Q. You'll find six groups of logs now in the form of jasper and agate, as well as a painted desert, in this Arizona national park. A. Petrified Forest

Q. The tallest known tree in the world is located in this national park along the California coastline. A. Redwood

Q. Rocky Mountain National Park is located in this state. A. Colorado

Q. Several High Sierra peaks, notably Mt. Whitney, are located in this California national park. A. Sequoia

Q. The Blue Ridge Mountains are the featured attraction of this national park headquartered in Luray, Virginia. A. Shenandoah

Q. The Little Missouri River badlands, the site of this former president's ranch, is now the site of a national park in North Dakota. A. Theodore Roosevelt

Q. You can explore ruins of colonial plantations and Carib Indian villages in this U.S. national park. A. Virgin Islands

Q. Voyageurs National Park, featuring ancient rock outcroppings, bogs, and many glacial lakes, is located near International Falls in this state. A. Minnesota

Q. Limestone caverns and large herds of bison are popular attractions at this South Dakota national park, headquartered in Hot Springs. A. Wind Cave

Q. This Alaskan national park is the largest in the United States, and contains the greatest concentration of mountains over 14,000 feet in the U.S. A. Wrangell–St. Elias

Q. You can find spectacular granite domes and monoliths, as well as the U.S.'s highest waterfall, in this national park. A. Yosemite

Q. Located in Springdale, Utah, this national park was given its name because Mormon settlers thought it was the promised land. A. Zion

JEOPARDY! BEHIND THE SCENES

In the other sections of the book, I focus on how to get on the show and win. In this chapter, I want to answer some of the most frequently asked questions about the show and about what it's like to be *Jeopardy!* champion. Many of the questions I answer below were submitted to me via the Unofficial *Jeopardy!* Fan Club Web page, found at http://www.MindFun.com, which my wife and I maintain. I urge you to visit the site and submit your question about *Jeopardy!* if it is not answered here.

What is Alex really *like?*
I have to start with this one, the most frequently asked question of all. I should begin by admitting that, as contestants, we really did not get a chance to talk to Alex one-on-one much more than what is seen on the screen. The contestant coordinators and the show's producers are very strict with security and want to prevent even the appearance that Alex is favoring one contestant over another. Alex only comes onstage after the game begins and the contestants are announced, just as you see it at home. He leaves right after the camera cuts away at the end of the game. So we didn't become intimate friends, by any means.

But, from what I could tell, Alex seemed a genuinely pleasant fellow. During the commercial breaks and the breaks between games, Alex would often chat with the contestants about a range of topics, revealing that he does, in fact, know a great deal. Rumor has it that Alex once took, and passed, the *Jeopardy!* qualifying test. Also, he does have a philosophy degree from a well-respected Canadian college.

However, he is given the questions and answers the night before and gets to study them for the next day's shows. So his knowledgeable appearance on the show is part personal knowledge and part preparation. Also, at the beginning of Final Jeopardy!, you may notice a crowd around the contestants as they place their wagers. These people are not the contestants' family members, as some people have conjectured in e-mails to me, but technicians from the show who determine, from the wagers, what the scores of the contestants will be if they get the answer right and if they get the answer wrong. They write this material on an index card and submit it to Alex during the commercial break. Thus, although it appears that Alex is figuring out the contestants' scores in his head after their answers are revealed, he really is just reading them off the card.

Alex did reveal a mischievous streak during the commercial breaks. As I stated, *Jeopardy!* tapes five shows each day, two days a week. The crew attempts to tape the shows in "real time," meaning that they tape a game segment, wait for the commercial break, and then resume taping. This helps with the editing, they said. Thus, during the commercial breaks, Alex had a few minutes to chat with the audience, talk to the contestants, and subject his hard-working stage manager, John Lauderdale, to a good-natured ribbing. Mr. Lauderdale was in charge of making sure that all aspects of the show were working together during the taping, including Alex being at the right place at the right time.

Alex was simply amazing at waiting during commercial breaks until the last second before taking his "mark"; that is, the spot where he needed to be standing when shooting resumed. Alex would be chatting away with the audience as the stage manager announced how much time was left in the break. As the stage manager, with an increasing degree of alarm, announced that only thirty seconds, then twenty seconds, and then ten seconds remained, Alex would not budge. Only when the countdown reached three seconds did Alex start his glide across the stage, hitting his mark just as the stage manager got to zero. Without missing a beat, Alex started into a smooth "welcome back" to the home audience. It was actually quite amazing (and amusing)!

What happens during commercial breaks?

I was surprised by the role that Johnny Gilbert played in the studio. As the audience waited for the shows to start, Johnny gave a very funny and interesting presentation about how the show is shot, what the audience should do, and some *Jeopardy!* history. He also answered questions from the audience during the commercial break and let the audience know when they should applaud like crazy: on Daily Doubles, when a contestant ran a category, or at the start of the second half. As a viewer at home, I had no idea Johnny interacted with the audience this way.

The contestant coordinators come over to the podiums during commercial breaks to see if the players are doing okay, to give them a little encouragement, and to bring them some water in little paper cups. (I asked for Scotch but they said I'd have to supply that on my own.) Also, during the commercial break before Final Jeopardy! the staff does a very nice thing. They make all of the contestants write the beginning of the proper question for Final Jeopardy!, so that nobody forgets to put the response in the form of a question. For example, if the category is "Saints" and the correct response is going to be "St. Francis of Assisi," a coordinator will come over during the break and tell each player to write "Who is" at the top of his or her screen. They simply don't want the heartbreak of players losing because in their nervousness they failed to write their Final Jeopardy! response as a question.

What's it like to be the champ?

At first, being the *Jeopardy!* champ is surprisingly anticlimactic. After the game ends, if you have not yet played your fifth and final game, you are rushed back to the dressing room to change into your outfit for the next game. (Remember, *Jeopardy!* likes to preserve the illusion that the contestants are there all week.) You barely have fifteen minutes to savor your victory and change your clothes before you are rushed back out there to face your next two opponents. Once your winning streak ends, either by losing or by reaching your fifth win, the coordinators congratulate you, have you sign some papers, and basically show you the door. They have to rush back to set up the remaining games of the day.

One of the coordinators will walk you to a side door of the studio, congratulate you again, maybe pat you on the back, and then, click, the studio door closes behind you and that's it. There are no roaring crowds, ticker tape parades, or plush limos waiting for you. It's just you on an empty lot. When it happened to me after my five-game stint, I actually laughed out loud to myself at the suddenness of it. My first thought was of David Spade on *Saturday Night Life* saying, "Buh-bye now." It was worse for me because when I went out to *Jeopardy!*, I could not afford to bring anyone out with me, not even my wife. So it was just me, dying to tell everyone I knew that I was the *Jeopardy!* champ.

The problem is that you cannot tell anybody that you won. Your shows will usually not air until three months after they are taped, and you sign a document saying you will not tell anyone the outcome of any game until it airs. Actually, the coordinators will tell you that you can tell your family and close friends, just not the news media. They say this because one poor guy called them a month after his appearance begging them to let him tell his wife. He had not told her yet that he had won several times. The prize for being close-lipped, however, has to go to Ryan Holznagel, 1995 Tournament of Champions winner, who managed not to tell even his close family how he had done during the tournament. It was especially effective in his case because he was trailing going into Final Jeopardy! in every game that he won in the tournament. What a thrill it must have been for his family to see his tournament performance without knowing the outcome ahead of time.

Sometimes, even if you tell your family that you won, they might not believe you. Dave Sampugnaro, 1996's top regular-season money winner with $72,000, tells a story about a cousin of his turning to him while watching one of his games where he was trailing and asking him, "Are you sure you really won this thing?" Also, even though I had already told her that I had won, my grandmother got so nervous when watching my shows on TV that she had to leave the room whenever I fell behind. I had to keep reassuring her that I had really won. Other times, people will kind of guess that you won, like if you buy an entire house full of furniture with "no money down, no payments for one year" and you are unemployed.

Once the shows air, you will indeed be a celebrity for a little while. I was living in Cleveland, Ohio, when my five-game regular-season stint aired, and I quickly learned that people in Cleveland absolutely love it when someone from the city wins something. It does not matter whether you are the Cleveland Indians, the *Jeopardy!* champ, or that football team that used to play there; Cleveland loves a winner. In fact, when Matt Zielinski won the *Jeopardy!* teen tournament in 1995, he was on the front page of the newspaper and was named one of Cleveland's most interesting people. When it was my turn as champ, I was recognized and approached about five times a day at first, especially in Parma, which must have the nation's highest per capita *Jeopardy!* viewership. I got my name in the paper and even got to do three radio appearances with "Trapper," a local radio celebrity, which was a blast.

Do they really pay you all that money, and how'd you spend it all?

Just about when your fame starts to fade away, you get another *Jeopardy!* pick-me-up in the mail. About ninety days after your final regular-season episode airs, you will receive a check for your winnings. Yes, they do actually pay you the money, and they do take some money out for taxes. You might be surprised, however, to learn that you get the entire amount of your total winnings less only 7 percent for California income tax. You are responsible for paying the rest of the taxes on the money on your own. So do not blow all the money; save some to pay Uncle Sam. In the appendix, my wife and tax advisor Zana Holley will give you some handy hints on paying the taxes on your *Jeopardy!* money.

What a great feeling it was to deposit that *Jeopardy!* check. When I went to deposit my Tournament of Champions check for $93,000 at the bank, they naturally asked me where the money came from. When I told them, and they satisfied themselves that I did not fit the drug courier profile, they immediately sent over their investment counselors to see if I needed "help" with the money. I also got calls from several of the other investment companies in town. What I really wanted to do was convert it all to $20 bills, spread them all over the floor, and roll around in them for a while, but bank officials frown on that sort of thing.

In the end, with a small part of the money I bought a couple of beds, a new car, dressers, clothes, trips, computers, and books and saw lots of movies. I also did some prudent things with the money by investing some and paying off all my credit cards. But the thing I bought that I value the most was *time*, the one thing I never have enough of these days. I took ten months off from my legal career and spent it with my wife and two-year-old daughter. Together we spent a glorious summer at Camp Canadensis in Canadensis, Pennsylvania, where I was an assistant head counselor (the kids all called me "Jeopardy"), my wife taught reading to the kids, and my daughter thrived on the attention from her three hundred big brothers and sisters. When that was done, I spent a few carefree months in beautiful Gainesville, Florida, before starting work again. My wife and I had a blast, and it was simply an irreplaceable chance to build a bond with my daughter at one of the most crucial stages of her development. Now we are just like bread and butter.

What's next?

Like thousands of people out there, being in *Jeopardy!*—let alone winning—had been a lifelong fantasy of mine. I had played and watched the game since before I can remember, and guys like Frank Spangenberg, Bob Blake, and Chuck Forrest (three fearsome champions on the show) were household names around my house. Having fulfilled that dream, my only regret is that I probably will not get a chance to play anymore. I mean, it's not like there is a professional trivia circuit, where trivia stars tour the nation playing in PQA tournaments (Professional Quiz Association) for $700,000 purses. I also doubt Merv Griffin is going to let me on *Wheel of Fortune,* and I pretty much paid off all my *Debt,* so those shows are probably not realistic options.

So where can I set my competitive sights now? Well, did you know that the winner of the Pillsbury Bake-Off gets $1,000,000? I don't know a torte from a tortellini, but I'm sure going to learn. And I shouldn't have any trouble getting along with the host of the Bake-Off—who was none other than Alex Trebek in 1998. So, if I ever do win the Pillsbury Bake-Off, be sure to see my book, which will follow soon thereafter and be called *How to Get Into the Pillsbury Bake-Off...and Win!*

PAT YOURSELF ON THE BACK

By the time you've reached this section of the book, you have probably put in a great deal of time and effort. You are also probably starting to face the same fear that I, and probably everyone who prepares a lot for the show, faced. "What if I put in all of that work and lose?"

Alas, that is the negative side of *Jeopardy!* In every *Jeopardy!* game, two people's *Jeopardy!* fantasy is forever wiped out. And there are so many ways to lose on *Jeopardy!*—a tougher-than-expected Daily Double, a tricky Final Jeopardy!, an opponent with a hot buzzer finger, or simply categories that are bad for you. So is it really worth it go to all the trouble?

I think it is. Before you go out to the show, look back at the work you have done and pat yourself on the back. If you accomplished even one of the following, it has all been worth it:

- You learned about areas of knowledge you otherwise never would have.
- You set goals for yourself and met them.
- You faced your fear of failing head-on and went for something everybody else wanted too.
- You picked apart a set of tasks and strategized about how to best succeed at them.
- You practiced with discipline.
- You are willing to get up in front of millions and "strut your stuff."

The journey to a goal is sometimes more important than achieving the goal. With this as your guidebook, I hope your journey to *Jeopardy!* stardom will be fun, informative, and challenging. Good luck!

THE ULTIMATE TAX GUIDE FOR THE JEOPARDY! CHAMPION

BY ZANA HOLLEY*

Immediate Planning

First of all, you need to determine in which calendar year you will receive your *Jeopardy!* money. *Jeopardy!* pays champions their winnings ninety days after their last air date. So you may not receive the money until six months after you actually went to Culver City, California, and taped your show(s). You will be required to include the money in your income during the calendar year in which you get that hot check in your hands.

Having this knowledge ahead of time can allow you to shift your income. Suppose that ninety days after your last air date falls in late December. You have the option of receiving your check in either December or January because *Jeopardy!* can delay you another month if you request them to do so.

Looking ahead, if you're pretty certain that you will be in a lower tax bracket next year because you have decided to take the however, that if you are going to the Tournament of Champions, this might backfire if you win another $100,000, because you

---

*Ms. Holley graduated with honors from the University of Florida College of Law, where she was a research editor of the Florida Law Review. She is a former law clerk of Hon. Joseph Bartunek and a tax advisor for Jackson-Hewitt.

next year off from work and live off your *Jeopardy!* winnings, then you should choose to receive your check in January. Note, might have to claim both sets of winnings in the same tax year. Of course, at that point, you will have won a total of around $150,000, give or take, so you probably won't be very upset.

Withholding/Estimated Tax Payments

Jeopardy! does *not* withhold *any* federal income tax from your winnings! They do withhold California income tax, but we will talk about that later. Right now, I need to caution you not to immediately spend *all* of your winnings, because you will have to pay the federal income taxes by next April 15, at the latest.

The IRS requires that you pay in during the year taxes equivalent to what you owed last year. So get out last year's tax return and look at the Total Tax line (line 53 on the 1998 Form 1040). Then check with your employer to see how much is being withheld, and determine if your withholding is going to equal last year's Total Tax. If it is, then you won't have to pay any underpayment penalties. However, if you are working less because you have lots of *Jeopardy!* money to live off of and you want to travel the world or spend all of your time studying for the Tournament of Champions, then your withholding may not be enough.

If you are still working and your withholding won't be enough to cover last year's Total Tax, you should give your employer a new Form W-4, instructing him to withhold enough additional federal income tax to pay in an amount equal to last year's Total Tax. If you are not still working or are working only very little, then you should make a quarterly tax payment.

The quarterly tax payments are made four times a year, but you will only need to make one payment, because you are receiving all of your money in one lump sum. The payment dates are April 15, June 15, September 15, and January 15 of the following year. You should make your quarterly payment on the date that most closely follows when you received your check. Except if you receive your check between January 1 and 15, don't make the quarterly tax payment until April 15.

To make a quarterly tax payment, call 800-TAX-FORM and order a free copy of IRS FORM 1040-ES, Estimated Tax for Individuals. You can also download it off the Internet using your computer. The IRS's World Wide Web address is http://www.irs.ustreas.gov. If you want the IRS to fax the form to you, call (703) 368-9694.

Saving Some Money to Pay Any Outstanding Balance

Making sure that you have paid in tax payments to the IRS equivalent to last year's Total Tax saves you from any underpayment penalties, but you may still owe significantly more taxes than that, so you need to save some of your winnings. I recommend that you put at least 20 percent of your winnings into a certificate of deposit to save it until tax time. If you have state and local taxes to pay on your winnings, you may need to save as much as 35 percent of your winnings. Once the tax year is over and you have your taxes done, then you can withdraw any of the money that you don't owe the IRS and do with it what you like. Consider contributing any leftover money to a traditional IRA or 401(k) for you and your spouse. As I discuss later, such contributions could whack $1,400 off of your taxes!

Saving and Investing Through Retirement Accounts

Now that you have won a bunch of money on *Jeopardy!*, why not take advantage of the benefits of retirement accounts, such as 401(k)s and IRAs? These retirement accounts should really be called tax-reduction accounts. Once you calculate the amount of taxes you will save on your *Jeopardy!* money, you will be excited about contributing to them.

If you are a moderate income earner, you probably pay about

35 percent between federal and state income taxes on your last dollars of income (I am referring to the marginal tax rate or tax bracket). Thus, with most of the tax-deferred retirement accounts, for every $1,000 you contribute into them, you save yourself about $350 in taxes in the year for which you make the contribution. Contribute $4,000 and whack $1,400 off your tax bill. This is true as long as you don't have a pension, because then you qualify for a traditional IRA tax deduction. Some taxpayers with pensions also qualify for this deduction. It depends on your income. This is also true for 401(k) contributions because they're made with pre-tax dollars.

After your *Jeopardy!* money is placed in a retirement account, any interest, dividends, and appreciation add to the amount of your account without being taxed until they're actually withdrawn. You get to defer taxes on all the accumulating gains and profits until you withdraw the money, presumably in retirement. Thus, more money is working for you over a longer period of time.

If you (or your spouse) are not an active participant in any retirement plan, then your IRA contributions are fully deductible, up to $2,000 for each of you. Plus, you have until April 15 each year to make your contribution for the previous year. So you can wait until you prepare your taxes and see how much you will owe if you contribute to an IRA and how much you will owe if you don't. Once you do this calculation, you will surely be picking up the phone to call your favorite mutual fund for its IRA forms. If you don't already have a favorite fund, check out *Consumer Reports* and *Money* magazines. They both rank the best funds according to their returns and their riskiness.

Also, keep in mind that the 1997 tax law made significant changes to the IRA laws and options. Specifically, you may withdraw funds free of penalties for educational expenses or a home purchase. So the IRA is now much more than just a retirement account.

California's Tax Bite

As Mike said earlier, California takes its seven percent in state income tax withholding right off the top, before you even get the check. But make sure you file a non-resident California return if you are not a resident. They're available on the Internet. Chances are that you will get a healthy refund. Also, do not forget that you can offset your federal tax liability with the California taxes you paid by using your California refund to help pay your federal tax bill. If you file California taxes early in February, you'll probably get the refund before April 15.

Conclusion

Despite our best efforts, there really is no way around paying a great deal of taxes on your *Jeopardy!* winnings. In fact, Mike paid enough taxes on his winnings to buy one of those brand-new Chevy Tahoes they give away to five-time winners on the show now. But as I said before, after Mike won $166,401 just for playing a game, it was hard to be bitter about it.

ABOUT THE AUTHOR

Michael Dupée is an attorney, physicist, computer programmer, Webmaster, and author living in Gainesville, Florida. A graduate of Emory University and the University of Florida College of Law, Mike represented both schools in College Bowl Academic Tournaments around the country. A lifelong trivia fan, Mike has been collecting trivia for over twenty years and won the 1996 *Jeopardy!* Tournament of Champions. He is also the author and programmer of an award-winning trivia Web site at http://www.MindFun.com and the author and editor of numerous articles in various legal periodicals. When he's not writing, programming, or giving legal advice, Mike enjoys spending time with his wife, Zana Holley, children Zadia and Spencer, and pets Misha and Petey.